Marie of Roumania

MABEL POTTER DAGGETT

Marie of Roumania

The Intimate Story of the Radiant Queen

By

Mabel Potter Daggett

Author of "Women Wanted," "In Lockerbie Street"

George H. Doran Company
On Murray Hill : : *New York*

"Cotroceni Palace,
Roumania,
Sept. 24, 1926.

"I am so happy. It is wonderful how you have been writing about me. And I thank you with all my heart for giving your people such a fine idea of the far-off Queen. I only hope they will not be disappointed with *real* me when I come along. When I look in on you in your New York I have a photograph of Ileana with the gypsies I want to give you, remembering how when you were in Roumania, the gypsies always interested you. I sail on October 12th. All my best wishes."

Marie

*From a letter of Her Majesty
to Mrs. Daggett.*

Contents

Marie of Roumania
The Intimate Story of the Radiant Queen

MARIE OF ROUMANIA

CHAPTER I

A Close-up on a Queen

IT seemed that I had stepped from the Orient Express right off into Once-upon-a-time and Long-ago. I rubbed my eyes like Alice in Wonderland. Still the shine did not come off.

The room into which a lady-in-waiting had ushered me was all golden—all the vine-sculptured walls of it, all the arched and vaulted ceiling of it, all the tables and chairs and cabinets of it. Everything was literally overlaid with gold leaf.

There were hanging, swinging lamps of gold and silver, curiously wrought. There were bowls of gold and copper and bronze everywhere filled with flowers. And the flowers—goldenrod and golden glow and marigold and purple asters. There was a divan covered with silken stuffs of gold and purple, with pillows on it in purple and all the shades of gold from palest yellow to orange gold. The carpet was of thick velvet in a rich orange tone. And all of the precious stuffs that streamed down to it from divan and luxurious easy chairs all draped in gold seemed blending their golden shades together to meet at last in this deep soft gold I felt beneath my feet.

Jeweled, stained-glass, casement windows stood ajar to let the sunlight in. From ancient forests outside was wafted the delicious fragrance of fir and spruce. And I noticed how the trees lifted their dark green tops directly against the blue of the heaven that arched so close above this high tower room.

Then a door in the golden wall opened. There was the sound of a vibrant step that came with happy haste. Now the golden room was all aglow as with a vivid magnetic presence. "Here I am," cried a voice with the eager joyful naïveté of a girl. And it was the Queen, with eyes as blue and hair as golden as any story book might tell. She was dazzlingly dressed. But most of all it was her pearls that one may never forget. I think they must be priceless.

But I did not find her, you see, as perhaps you would have expected a Queen to be, sitting on her throne. That is at the palace in Bucharest. This where we were, a lovely castle in the Carpathian mountains, is the summer royal residence. Nor was she wearing, either, her robes of ermine. All the same, she was radiantly apparelled without benefit of any such symbols of state. And she came tripping right down a shaft of sunlight that splashed the room with its final touch of splendor.

She was in the gorgeous embroidered national

costume of her own Roumanian peasant people. Bound round her white brow and floating in long lace ends behind, she wore the *marama*, as the headdress of soft tissue is called. She had on the white tunic of the same material, intricately stitched with silks in red and blue and gold in a very old pattern. It was further ornamented down the front and on the deep full sleeves of it with gold sequins that shone and sparkled with her every movement. Over this tunic she wore the *fota*, the short kilted skirt of brilliant red homespun. It was heavy with gold embroidery as thickly laid on as if modeled and sculptured on the cloth. And it was all so heavily golden that above her white silk-clad ankles and her red-slippered feet, it swung as she walked with a certain rhythm, keeping time too with her swinging necklaces of pearls.

So she made a splendid figure, oriental surely and almost barbaric in her beauty. But fairy tale-like as she appeared, she was all real beside. With the cordial clasp of a firm white hand, she instantly set aside all formality. It is so sovereign a gesture as it must be few monarchs might make. All of the things to be done when one comes before a Queen, all of the things I didn't know at all about—well, anyhow, she made me feel I needn't do them. There was royal absolution from every rite in the way she threw herself full length on the divan that streamed with precious stuffs of gold and silver. Into the luxurious depths of the cushioned chair placed for me beside it, I could sink comfortably too, all anxious forebodings of form and ceremony forgotten.

"Have a cigarette," she said, snapping open a golden jeweled case. She lighted one for herself. And we took up time where last we had left it. That was at the peace conference in Paris. Perhaps you recall those days? How when men had made the war, in every land the cry was raised, Women Wanted! And women came to load freight cars, and to mine coal and to make munitions, and to drive ambulances under shrapnel fire. But after the war was over and men would make the peace, they meant to make it alone. And they did, but for just one woman only.

"Why, what in the world have you come for?" they asked in startled surprise one day. And they lifted their gaze in amazement, those gentlemen there at the peace table in Paris. Just among themselves, you know, they were picking up the pieces of civilization to patch together a new map of the world.

"Sirs," Queen Marie had answered demurely, "I have come to give Roumania a face in the affairs of nations."

It had been afterward as we sat together on a sofa at the Ritz Hotel in this Paris, that she told me. England, she pointed out, had its Lloyd George. America had Wilson. France had Clemenceau. So land after land was being envisaged to the public through a personality that made its own people's propaganda. Therefore

16

she had come, as she so frankly and engagingly announced, to give Roumania a face.

And she did. Who so much as knew before where on the map this Roumania was? But from the time of the lady's dramatic arrival in Paris, it has been reckoned with. Such a beautiful face it was that flashed into the newspapers' front pages, to hold ever since the admiring attention of two continents.

This then was the woman I had come far to see. Since our first meeting in that campaign that captured a peace conference, there had been royal crested letters that I treasure, signed "Yours in sincere friendship, Marie." And at last there was the invitation that had bidden me come to visit a Queen. That, you see, is the way it occurred. But how it all happened, I do not yet know. Nor, I think, does she. We have in common, well, a sense of humor, and of course our Anglo-Saxon tongue. The nationality that she has made famous is hers by marriage. The wife of King Ferdinand of Roumania, she is nevertheless herself by birth an English princess. She is, you see, the descendant of kings and kings. And I am the daughter of a revolution that would make all men equal. She is a ruler who believes in her right. Still, here we are in her golden room, aristocrat and democrat. The Queen is on her divan. I am sitting opposite in the deep, soft-cushioned chair. "It is strange, is it not?" I murmur. She nods assent.

Down below on the mountain side the monastery bells are pealing.

.   .   .   .

This at which I have arrived is a very old land. It is mystical with a religion that rises like incense from the hearts of a prayerful people. It is medieval with customs that still make decorative the everyday life of a primitive folk. The little town of Sinaia is called after the ancient monastery of the Greek orthodox church which has stood here for 400 years. And both were named for the even more ancient Sinaia in Arabia. Sinaia, in Roumania, on the route of the Orient Express which stops here some three hours before arriving at Bucharest, serves as the summer capital. Above the railroad station are great hotels and a casino and many white villas of the rich. High above them the monastery, orientally red and blue and golden, ornaments the mountain side. Through the arched entrance, beneath its black and gold-domed bell tower, you pass to the royal estate that reaches right up the wooded slopes to the snow capped mountain peaks. There is really a group of castles with their many turret; and steep gabled roofs, in Nuremburg style, white plastered, timbered with heavy carved oak. Before them are wide terraces brimming with bright flowers and set with sculpture and with fountains of silvery falling water.

To reach the royal residence, you must have credentials. Every now and then through the forest, even after you have successfully passed the monastery gate, a guard with gun and bayonet steps out from a sentry box to challenge in Roumanian, Who goes there? Castle Pelash was the residence of old King Carol who built all of these castles in his day. There he lived with his wife, Elizabeth, known to the world as Carmen Sylva. Since the death of the former rulers, it is used by the present king for his offices, for the assembling of the Crown Council and for official and state entertainments. Castle Pelasor, meaning little Pelash, occupied as the present royal family's residence, is less austere in its grandeur. And the personal apartments of the Queen, as you see in the golden room, are most artistically designed and executed. In still another smaller castle on the mountain side lived the Crown Prince Carol and his wife, the Crown Princess Helene, with the future heir to a throne, the laughing golden-haired baby, little Prince Mihai.

Here at Sinaia I found life lived colorfully. Night and day before the entrance to Castle Pelasor there is a guard of four armed soldiers always at such very stiff attention that they seem like statues standing there. The porter who so silently swings back the great castle door looks just as a real retainer should. He is a very large man with a very long black beard. And his blue coat that hangs to his heels is trimmed with beautiful bands of embroidery glittering with the royal crest. Three times a day a bugler, stepping before the castle entrance, sounds the call for meals and the assembling of the court. In the castle's audience chamber, the company arrives to do obeisance before their sovereigns. There are princes and princesses and almost always some visiting minister of state and a gold-braided general or two. And there are the aides-de-camp of the King's retinue and the ladies-in-waiting for the Queen, who make so much of the majesty that hedges about a throne. Every one must be on time. Our eyes are on the clock. Suddenly all conversation abruptly ceases. There is a little expectant hush. At precisely the appointed moment a door opens. The King in military uniform, with sword at his side, is entering from his apartment. And down the main staircase, in her bright embroideries and short swinging skirt, comes the Queen.

Now each member of the assembled company, according to rank and importance, steps forward and, bowing very low, kisses the hand, first of the King and then of the Queen. I am with the ladies-in-waiting. Each of them as she bends the knee makes a queer, quick little dip, "dropping a curtesy." But this is an art that one must be born to. I knew if I tried it, I'd fall on my face. I think the Queen did too. Suppressing the merriment in her eyes, she fixed it all that first day when I came along. With quick tact she had shaken hands. So always the King did too.

Still there is more. Now each gentleman present

must kiss each lady's hand. I had never before seen anything like that done except on the stage. The first time it happened to me, I gave a little start. Eventually, however, I came to stand for it without jumping. It was three times a day, you know. So one got over the surprise. When all ceremonial observances had been completed, the court passed into the dining room, the King and Queen leading the way. The royal household, however, varied. Often, as when I had first arrived, the King was gone a-hunting. Sometimes Carol with his Princess was present. Little girl portraits of two daughters looked down from the dining room wall; one is the wife of the King of Serbia and the other married the King of Greece. Prince Nicholas, the second son, getting his training in the English navy, was home on a two weeks' leave. Princess Ileana, the youngest of the family, was traveling with her governess in France.

But there were two young visitors: Prince Gottfried Hohenlohe, the Queen's nephew, is the son of her sister who made a German marriage; and Archduchess Marie, her niece, is a daughter of the sister who married the Russian Grand Duke Cyril. Friedel and Mashka, every one called them. Mashka was only seventeen. But she was darkeyed, full-red-lipped, deep-bosomed, and very handsome. With it all, she had the frankness and sincerity of a child.

"I don't care at all for society and for great

palaces," she told a visiting diplomat one day. "But I just love the country."

"And what, then, is your ambition in life?" he asked.

"To get married and have a great many children," said Mashka quite simply.

"I hope that you may attain your wish," smilingly replied the statesman. He bowed low and kissed her hand.

And, "Thank you," Mashka answered gravely.

Friedel was at that age when he had just passed through his first love affair. He was being subjected to the customary royal régime for recovery, sent on a visit to forget. Always Mashka and Friedel were asking me of America. "Perhaps you may both come there some day," I said.

"But I am German. Who in America would wish to see me?" the boy answered sorrowfully.

"Why, the war is over," I exclaimed. "Everybody can be friends."

"Can we, do you think?" There was such eager pathos in Friedel's tone. "Everybody in the world? Can we be friends again, even if I am German . . ." The young voice trailed off with such wistful sweetness.

Mashka and Friedel and I became very well acquainted. Because, when all around us were speaking Roumanian or sometimes French, we could talk English together. How blest is that tie that binds you may never know until you have presented yourself at court so scantily equipped with language that you can rely upon only your mother tongue.

"Where is your French?" Beneath the searching gaze of the ladies-in-waiting, I felt like a Bolshevik who had broken into the royal preserves. Certainly I was not in right. French is the passport to polite society in Europe. Every one who speaks anything else speaks also French as a matter of course and as the current medium of communication. At a royal court, which is the politest place of all, it is indispensable.

"Where is your French?" repeated the ladies-in-waiting. They became, I believe, not only suspicious but at last curiosity was mingled too with scorn. "What do they teach you over there? Don't you learn anything at all at school?" At least through the medium of their sort of English and my scanty French, I could gather that was the way they felt in Roumanian.

"I had it," I insisted desperately, as vainly I grasped at memory for my far-away college French. There was Latin and Greek I believe I could conjugate still. But these were dead languages. It was a living language I required. And it would not come.

Oh, of course, "Bonjour" and "Je ne parle Français" and a few little things like that I managed to bring to the surface. But even if I could have done them all, those sentences in which I was once 100 percent, they would not have sufficed for this environment. "See the girl sitting there." "The boy has a new book." Those are not really useful remarks at all. Anything I could possibly have commanded would have been utterly inadequate. So I found myself in this Roumanian world, in a crisis quite cut off from communication. And the crisis came.

First I should tell you that the importance of French at court is all the more important because of the importance of a lady-in-waiting. The Queen has four of them. Three are white-haired. There is one who is not. And she has lovely dark eyes. It was she who was going to teach a handsome visiting Englishman to speak Roumanian. "We shall begin with the verb *to love*," she said. "And you will learn." I think he did.

Now, all of the ladies-in-waiting belong to the very oldest Roumanian nobility. It is the highest honor that can come to them, this, to be selected for the service of the Queen. Two of them are in residence with their own apartments at the castle. And two more are always ready to come on call. Their place is neither that of companion nor social secretary. But it is both of these and then a good deal more glorified. They travel with the Queen and receive with the Queen. They "hold audiences" for the Queen, which she may not have the time or the inclination to hold herself. They are the special consultants of the Queen. Through them she both receives messages and transmits her wishes. And with the wide French atmosphere with which they encircle her, they become, as it were, the special guardians of all approach to the throne. Each wears on the front of her gown as a badge of office a diamond monogrammed letter M, for Marie, surmounted by a diamond crown.

Of course I saw how much I ought to speak French. When I couldn't, the ladies-in-waiting kindly did what they could with English as from day to day they arranged the royal appointments for my program. They were very polite. But now and then I think they must have said in Roumanian to themselves, "Oh, bother." Because you see it was often difficult. To speak a foreign language is not at all the same thing as to talk it. Each of us often quite missed the other's meaning.

Which was how I came to make my real *faux pas*. A lady-in-waiting had come for me to spend the morning with the Queen. It was to be a whole morning in the golden room. And it would be lovely.

Just outside the door she paused for some further instructions: there would be at one o'clock a "big lunch." That much I gathered. Some more I didn't get. But a "big lunch" was certain to be at the other castle where I didn't yet know the way. Would she then be coming to pick me up?

But the door of the golden room was even now opening. And I was in the presence of the Queen. Always when I crossed this threshold, a dream closed round me. And the morning had gone when the Queen herself brought us both back to reality. She looked at her watch with a start: "Why, that luncheon!" she exclaimed. "Oh, I meant to tell you too," she hurriedly added, "that the King is coming to-day. And I awfully hope he will like you."

It was seven minutes to the hour for a luncheon like that. The Queen, of course, was ready in her embroidered costume for any castle occasion. But I must dress. I rushed from the golden room, my one thought first to find the lady-in-waiting. Else, how should I know how to reach the luncheon? From the Roumanian servants I might not even enquire the way. The great castle? And this was the "little" one. Even here, you've no idea how many doors a castle can have. Once the lady-in-waiting, taking me up one long corridor and down another, had pointed out hers: "There," she had said, "I shall be if you need me."

Where now was the door that belonged to the lady-in-waiting? This, it must be, I decided, making desperate selection. I knocked. It was too timidly. I knocked louder.

And the door opened. A valet held it wide, oh, so wide! And silhouetted against the light directly behind him was a gentleman just slipping into a dress shirt.

For one terrible instant I stood transfixed. And the gentleman did too, head forward, arms just thrust through the sleeves of the shirt. And the valet did too, hand on the still wide-open door. Then I found my English excuses. And fled.

Somehow I reached my own right room. How

I had missed my guide I never did learn. After all, you know, she was the Queen's lady-in-waiting, not mine. And finding me late, I suppose she had hurried along in the royal train.

I had just about three minutes to spare for dressing. Where was that beautiful gown I had brought for just such an occasion as this? I tried to think. Why, to be sure, just where it would most naturally be, all snug in tissue paper packing at the bottom of my trunk.

Three minutes! And now there were only two. That lovely thing in orchid satin and lace! I never could dig it out. With bitter resignation I swung open a closet door, to grab the nearest gown within reach, gray and from the year before last. I had acquired my underslip and was struggling with suede slippers when there came a knock at the door. Something in French was said in a masculine voice. "Wait, please wait," I begged in English.

And then, oh, this was the gown that fastened in back. However should I get it done? Again the knock at the door. The voice this time was imperative, absolutely so. I just felt it was saying, "The King commands."

That surely was in effect its message. I had succeeded with one fastening at the top of the dress and one at the middle, you know. At the next knock I had to open the door. The gentleman who was there was an aide-de-camp and with expression and tone so anxious and urgent that there was

no doubt he was telling me I should come immediately. What is that of which one may be guilty?
Lèse majesté, I feared. My right hand behind me
frantically clutched my gown together. But even
so, of course I went.

I found indeed a "big lunch" for which the
King had specially returned. The greatest dignitaries of the eastern church were here, with long
black beards and high black hats and long black
robes. They had come not merely from nearby
Bucharest. Metropolitans from Alexandria and
Antioch and a Patriarch from Jerusalem were
here.

They had come officially to inaugurate the King
and Queen as Defenders of the Faith. Roumania,
now large enough and important enough, so suc-
ceeds to the position formerly held by great Russia.
With solemn ceremony in the Crown Council
Chamber, the King and the Queen were decorated
each with a great gold chain and an enormous
splendid jeweled cross.

All of which had been completed before I had
arrived. The aide-de-camp who had rushed me
across from Pelasor and along the graveled paths
and up the staircase of Pelash had just time to
hurry me into position in the line of gentlemen and
ladies-in-waiting and others who stood outside the
Council Chamber.

Fortunately I found myself beside a friend.
"Oh, Mashka," I cried, turning round and letting

go the frantic clutch at my gown, "could you button me up?"

She did, with some giggling but with real celerity. Then the doors of the Council Chamber had opened and the procession, led by their Majesties, appeared.

Mashka whispered: "I've got hysterics in my hind legs. And see how cold my hands are! It's the way I always get when anything important occurs."

But now behind the last military commander and minister of state, we too who had waited outside closed in to follow on to the great state dining hall. It was a very splendid luncheon with all the gold plate and the jeweled goblets. There must have been, I should say, some fifty guests. Just after the caviar I looked up to catch the rather intent gaze of a black-frocked gentleman directly across the table. Such handsome dark Roumanian eyes! He was smiling ever so little.

Oh! Now I knew. Where had I seen those eyes? Why, just above the neckband of the gentleman's union suit as, head bent forward, he recently stood poised in struggle with his shirt.

Now the embarrassment of that previous painful moment it would not have been possible to continue. So I smiled. And he smiled again, now quite frankly.

Still the incident didn't close. Pretty soon I noticed a humorous expression more or less rippling up and down the table. The King had leaned forward a little, with a look down my way. Even a Metropolitan was smiling. And what was the matter with Friedel? His napkin before his face, he was choking with either a fishbone or laughter.

After the luncheon, everybody gathered in the beautiful audience chamber of great Castle Pelash. All of the most important people, you see, in this part of the world were here. And I was here, in the gown of the year before last, feeling just as wilted as a woman would.

Still, right like that, it had to be. The Queen was now presenting me to His Majesty, the King.

He shook hands with me, it did seem, cordially. And it was nice of the Queen. To make everything quite easy, she laid her hand confidentially on the King's sword hilt: "I want you, my dear," she said, "to tell Mrs. Daggett all about the Roumanian kolchak, the pink crocus that grows in the meadows, because you know so much about botany."

Still, the King, it appeared, could not be interested in the pink kolchak. They had told me what a shy man he is. But now he plunged right in, as it were, and with a wide-open smile. "Mrs. Daggett," he said, "I understand has been having adventures in Roumania. Right here at Pelasor."

So then the story was out. The royal remark seemed to ring round the audience chamber. A little smiling circle was closing about us. On the outer edge of it, the gentleman with the handsome Roumanian eyes shook his head. It was not he who had told.

Ah, Friedel! Now he was amplifying and explaining for the edification of all who understood English. It appeared that many did.

"You see," said Friedel, "my room was next. So I could hear it all. I grasped perfectly just how much Mrs. Daggett needed help. But I couldn't make a move. I was worse off even than was Prince X——. I hadn't yet reached my shirt. So I just got behind my door and stayed there."

The next day the Queen said to me with relief: "It seems that the King likes you very well." And I found myself seated next His Majesty at table. One may get over, then, even a gown of year before last. And a *faux pas* can have a happy ending.

Breakfast at the royal castle was at nine promptly. No, not in bed. At the table. And the Queen was always there. There were times when the household had retired very late. There had been perhaps a musicale in the audience chamber with artists up from Bucharest. Or it had been just the Queen and I together in the Golden Room until the hours had slipped past midnight.

Now, I would think, as I opened my own sleepy eyes to make haste in the morning, surely *now* she will be napping. But she never was. The Queen is the busiest woman I know. Her day begins at 7 A. M. with her correspondence. Beginning soon after breakfast, there are dignitaries and deputations to be received in audience more or less all day. In the evening there are frequent social affairs that engage the royal attention often up to midnight. But there are intervals between when all these affairs cease from troubling. "We shall be going now," she said one day, "to visit my people."

Religion and royalty afford for the Roumanian peasant the rich display that decorates drab existence. But the Mother of God can be seen only as a pictured ikon. The Queen is Our Beautiful Lady, who from her high and splendid places every once in a while comes down to earth.

So now at the Sinaia railroad station they opened the royal waiting room and spread the red velvet carpet. And we all passed through to the royal train, the Queen and Mashka and the lady-in-waiting and I and some visitors from the English nobility. The stateroom which I had was done in mahogany with green velvet hangings and carpet and the royal crest embroidered on the pillows. And there was a lounge outside with library table and divan. The Queen's own car has polished mahogany woodwork inset with ebony and inlaid with mother of pearl. Her bedroom has the walls all covered with moss green velvet and there are touches of gold embroidery. Her sitting room is hung and upholstered in pale blue silk brocade.

The railroad time-table, specially printed for *Tren Regale* in letters of gold, outlined a trip of four days. The train traveled always at night. In the morning, after breakfast in the dining car, we invariably found ourselves arrived at a station fluttering with flags in the Roumanian red, yellow and blue and palpitant with the excitement of a festive occasion. The people had been holding their places in line for hours. Nearly always too there were soldiers with glittering officers to emblazon the scene. And there were town folk in modern store clothes. But the real color note was set by those others: women with kerchief-covered head and wearing the embroidered blouse and homespun skirt; men in tight white woolen trousers, embroidered white sheepskin vests and high black sheepskin hats; then there were the children, quaint miniatures of their elders.

I looked out over these, her people. How eager each upturned face! At the moment of her appearing, you could note a quick little intake of the breath like a little gasp of joy. Then into all the dark eyes came exactly the look they have in church.

The Queen stood forth sparkling in all of her embroideries. She was smiling, happy, herself as joyous as the throng she looked down upon. This, you could see, was just as much her day as theirs. Then at a signal from the schoolmaster, the assembled worshippers below broke forth in song. And there thrilled out on the morning the wildly beautiful strains of the national anthem, the "Traiasca."

Always they had spread their most beautiful carpet and strewn it with flowers. On this the Queen stepped down from the train. A little girl

33

presented a bouquet of flowers. The mayor, with official red sash worn diagonally across his breast, made a speech and knelt and kissed his sovereign's hand. So did the generals and the colonels and the black-robed priests.

At the end of the carpet of flowers, a fragrant evergreen triumphal arch lifted the words wrought in flowers, "Bine ati venit," which is literally, "Well have you come." Beneath this we followed the Queen to the waiting automobiles. As we passed, scores of eager outstretched hands reached for the picture postcards of the beautiful face, as the lady-in-waiting scattered these souvenirs of the day. Even the royal hand scattered some too.

Amid wild cheering and cries of "Long life," we were off. Riding beside the car in which I sat with the Queen, galloped the convoy of outriders, sometimes as many as ten or twenty, each sashed diagonally with a bright embroidered band. Always there was such a guard of honor to accompany us for a mile or so beyond the town.

Then we went on our way for the day to find the far little villages. Sometimes for lunch we stopped beside the road and the servants brought out the hamper that had come from the train. There was a careful survey of the landscape. One green mound and another was looked at. "No, here it would be nicest, beneath this larch tree," Mashka called. The laprobe from the car was spread. And a Queen, tucking her red-slippered feet beneath her, sat comfortably down on the ground to picnic with the rest of us on cold chicken and bread and butter and pickles and layer cake. But sometimes we lunched more grandly, when we were entertained at the great estates of the nobility.

When our car had swept through the gates and up to the door, there met the Queen, as she ascended the steps, the master of the house himself, bearing a silver salver from which she dipped a piece of bread in salt and ate. It is a very old ceremony of hospitality. Then on crested china that proclaimed the family's very old nobility was served a royal feast indeed with pâté-de-fois gras and caviar and everything rare that might be set before a Queen. They were very much honored to have her there. They too kissed her hand and in their manner was all the charm of old-time grace and courtesy.

But it was among the humble folk I liked best to see her royalty register. How they had learned I do not know, but every little village surely had heard she was coming. Each little thatched-roof cottage had been specially made all glorious, with the bright banners of their beautiful homemade rugs flung in gay salutation from every window and balcony. Always there was the triumphal evergreen arch of welcome for her to pass under, while along the little curving crooked street an adoring population lined up, bowed and bowed and bowed in welcome and cheered and cheered "Long Life." Sometimes we went through with a

35

wave of her white hand. But where there would be a lovely old monastery that the centuries had left, we always stopped.

And as the Queen in her beauty stepped from the car, the people pressed forward. Not just ceremoniously, but passionately they kissed her hand. Young people in their joy began to dance the Hora to the strains of a flute.

Some one always ran ahead to set the monastery tower bell ringing. At the outer porch of the church there would be the priest in his vestments presenting a shining cross for the Queen to kiss. Then inside, with all the people coming too but standing respectfully back, the Queen would inspect and admire exquisite ikons, old embroideries, and rare carpets.

Last of all, while the frescoed saints looked very softly down, the priest would show for her to see the dearest treasure, the silver-bound copy of the sacred gospels. In the hush that followed, the Queen led the way and we stepped out as quietly as we could, one by one, past the people who waited in silence.

As twilight fell we always turned back, speeding along the dusty road to the royal train again. Every cottage window had a lighted candle placed in greeting. Again whole villages called "Long life!" And literally they blanketed the royal car with the flowers they flung as we flew by.

At dinner on the train on the last night of the trip, there sat at the head of the table a very radiant Queen. She seemed to sparkle more than ever in her embroideries and the beautiful face flushed pink as a girl's: it was, you see, the effect of all the adoration that had risen like incense before her shrine. "We've had a lovely time," she declared, "haven't we?"

. . . .

Among all of the royal palaces and castles there is one that is very special. And that not only in Roumania. There is in all Europe no other royal residence so romantic. Castle Bran is in the far fastnesses of the Carpathians. It stands right against the sky, rising precipitately out of the very crown of a mountain peak. The name means a "gate" and it is so called because it guards the mountain pass below. This is the very old fortress with which the Saxons defended this part of Europe against the Turks. Inscriptions on its foundations show that it stood here in the year 1200, and how much older than that it may be no one can tell. This ancient fortification, presented by the city of Brasov to the Queen, she has restored and furnished and made her beautiful Castle Bran. There are apartments for the King and for each of the children as they may come for a visit. Still this is her personal castle. "There is no court," she explained to me, "not even a lady-in-waiting. And I ask here only the people I like."

It is to Castle Bran that the Queen turns for escape from all affairs of state. From Sinaia, Bran is distant some three hours' journey by automobile, so that you may go and return in a day. We went, the Queen and Mashka and I, in her polished mahogany, silver-mounted Rolls-Royce car. The top is always down and she rides with the wind. Peasants' straw-covered carts, and flocks of sheep and herds of goats made way. Pigs and chickens and geese scattered to the ditch as we flew by. Flashing here through a village and there through a forest, over a mountain and down to a valley, the beautiful machine seemed to rise and dip like a bird. And at last with one final whirl straight for the clouds, it had dropped us at the castle entrance. Up so high, there never was need for a moat.

A narrow flight of some thirty steps leads to the great oak door. When you stand in the ancient courtyard, you know you have come to the Castle of Dreams-Come-True, the mystical, enchanted Castle of Dreams-Come-True.

You lift your eyes to high gray towers, hung with red-roofed, brown-timbered balconies blazing with flowers in orange and crimson. Now these balconies do not run regularly. Sometimes one slips behind a gray embrasure to emerge again farther on. And sometimes one drops a step or two or three. But up and down and around as they go, there are two of them. From the courtyard the most fascinating little narrow old stone staircases wind mysteriously up and away into the interior of the castle.

Try to follow one and it leads you maybe up to some high landing where you bend beneath a low arched doorway and brush past a sculptured saint in a niche in the wall; and lo, now where is your staircase? When you come to it again, it may be another that has wandered up this way from the opposite tower.

I gave up trying to count the staircases. They say there are seven. Choose any one you will, and it brings you to a new surprise. Any room you reach will always be along some narrow ledge and then up a step or two or down a step or two from any other. There are plain whitewashed walls and dark timbered ceilings and sometimes the very same little old windows from which those crusading knights in armor looked out on their other centuries. This simple background is made to glow with richly colored rugs and rare hangings. The furniture is all of quaint design, some of it collected from Europe's bygone ages and some of it built right here as the mistress of this castle has directed. "This is the way we will have that cupboard," she said to her architect, with a few quick lines of her pencil on paper. And so it was done.

There is everywhere through the castle majestic beauty, solemn and ancient and old. And then a charm so subtle I could not withal define its mystery. Until later the Queen herself was telling me: "You see, I have given my castle a soul."

That it is which makes all the other royal residences you can see in Europe, compared with hers, seem like museums. They are repositories for objects of art, more costly perhaps than her smaller kingdom may afford. But as houses where people live, they utterly lack the feeling motif you find in hers. Most of all, at Bran there is that sense of a woman's presence that lingers in every room. Even if you should not see her at all, you would say with conviction, "I know that surely at least yesterday she went through that open door." Especially there are flowers everywhere to smile that she has been here.

"You have to have flowers," says the Queen, "to make a house come alive." All of the low white-washed rooms are splashed with their color. They hang in swinging Roumanian kettles from the ceiling. They stand in high Bessarabian jars against the walls. Bowls from Ragousa hold them; brass pots from Constantinople, and glass vases from Venice hold them. There are even pools of flowers in low flat dishes set on the floor. I have never seen anything more decorative than a dark Spanish brazier afloat with flaming bunches of nasturtiums placed just where a stream of sunlight slanting over the floor sets it all afire.

Flowers in just such profusion you will see in every residence that the Queen of Roumania occupies. At Bran there are the saints besides. In an angle of a room, at a turn of a corridor, you may meet them anywhere in sudden surprise. Sometimes they are high carved wooden figures, sometimes little sculptured ones set in a niche in a wall. Some are the very Madonnas the crusaders worshipped. And all are worn and very old with the far-off ages from which they have traveled down. But they never strayed here by chance, I said to myself. Some one who liked them asked them here. And just then with a smile and a wave of her hand, the Queen introduced them: "My people, you see, who live with me."

We sat on the high flowered balcony at dinner. "There's going to be such a beautiful storm," the Queen announced, "we shall not go back to-night." She turned to me: "That will not matter. I shall lend you a nightgown." She said it as casually as any other woman. "And I shall put you to sleep, let me see, I think in the bedroom of my Ileana."

Hardly had we finished coffee, when suddenly from over the next mountain with a mighty rush and a roar the storm had come. Now there is no such thing as electric light at Bran. In the central castle hall, Florentine silver lamps swing softly in the gloom. On the white Roumanian hearth, for this cool evening a fire glowed red from out the farthest blackness. Lightning flashed. The thunder rolled. The wind howled. But the Queen stretched herself at ease on a divan and smiled: "This, my castle," she explained, "is the house where the four winds meet. But its walls are four feet thick."

At the next resounding crash, Mashka had covered her ears. "But," the Queen insisted quietly, "it's only God. It is God warning us what he can do. That's the way I always feel. In a

41

storm at Bran, all the mystery of God and the majesty of God just sweep surging through my soul."

Still Mashka crouched all the evening on the great bear rug on the floor until at last the storm had gone rumbling on its way across mountain and valley.

It was eleven o'clock. "And now it is time for good night," said the Queen. She held high against the shadows a lighted silver candlestick her maid had brought. She stepped to the wall beyond the bookcases. A paneled door flew open at her touch. From the threshold she waved her hand to us.

And she had disappeared down the secret staircase in the thick stone wall. Armored knights once clattered down these same stone steps to dark dungeons where they led. This is later by some seven hundred years. And a Queen in red-slippered feet steps softly down to pleasant dreams in a beautiful chamber.

I awoke next morning with that feeling one sometimes has, you know, of left-over wonder. My hand brushed the spread of rich yellow satin. The light streamed through curtains of orange silk at the window. And from a picture on the wall, the saint for whom Ileana is named looked down at me. Ah yes, I remembered. I had slept in the bed of a princess. And I had worn the Queen's lace nightgown.

. . . .

The next day, back at Sinaia again, the chime of the monastery bells drifted softly through the golden tower room. The Queen was on her divan. And I was in the deep soft easy chair. Often I had noticed the bracelet she wore on her wrist, a bracelet of pearls and diamonds from which hung a tiny golden key. Always she wore it as we walked in the garden or strolled in the forest together, as also when she dressed for the grandest functions of state. What might its meaning be?

This day on a small table beside the divan I observed a book bound all in gold. Purposely, of course, it was there. At length the Queen reached for it. I saw her unclasp the mysterious bracelet. Carefully she detached the tiny golden key. And with it she unlocked the golden clasp of the golden book. "It is," she explained, "the Book of my Memories. Only one other person, my most favorite lady-in-waiting, has ever seen what is written here. This key unlocks the book. The book never leaves my personal possession. And the key I wear night and day on my wrist."

Now there were hours in the golden room when we talked of many things. Of life and love, as women will. There were the times when we laughed together. And the times when we wept together. As women will. But more. There were the times when I would have hushed my very breathing: out of the golden book steadily, with even measured tones, Marie of Roumania was reading to me. And from a far little girlhood, through flaming youth and full maturity, a woman's soul was passing by.

So I came to know something of a life that has been lived with a great deal of joy, with some heartbreak, but always with very high courage.

How the monastery bells are pealing!

CHAPTER II

Born to the Purple

SHE is so very royal. Such an ancient lineage has gone to make her the ruler that she is. Saxon or Scythian, either or both, may be those blue eyes of hers. She is sprung from the two oldest courts of Europe. The two greatest empires of modern times produced her. And even while she was coming down the ages the greatest empire of ancient times was laying out the kingdom to which she would enter in.

On October 29, 1875, at Eastwell, Kent, in England, to Prince Alfred Duke of Edinburgh and his wife, Marie Alexandrovna, a child was born. They named her for a grandmother who was the Empress of Russia and a grandmother who was the Queen of England, Marie Alexandra Victoria. A brother, Alfred, who had preceded her, died in his youth. Three sisters followed her to be christened according to not infrequent royal custom, even in repetition, with significant family names: Victoria Melita, a year her junior, who is now Her Imperial Highness, wife of the Grand Duke Cyril of Russia, first cousin to the murdered Czar; Alexandra, about three years younger, who married Prince Hohen-

lohe of Wurtemberg, Germany; and Beatrice,
eight years after, who became her Royal Highness,
the wife of Prince Alfonso of Bourbon Orleans,
first cousin to the King of Spain.

Now none of these little girls ever was called
by the names that were written in the book of the
Church of England at the time of their baptism.
They found at home much simpler ones. And they
grew up familiarly as Missy and Ducky and
Sandra and Baby B. Even to this day the Queen
of Roumania is affectionately known among all the
royalties of Europe as just "Missy."

You see, there is somehow about her a quality
of eternal youth, which, no matter how much
majesty she may since have attained, still keeps her
enshrined as they long ago learned to love her.
And it is one of the things specially to be said about
her, that she has loved more and been loved more
than almost any other woman of her time.

For that, of course, the fairies who sponsored
her birth are responsible. They took counsel together. That they should dower the child richly,
it was quite agreed. "She shall have brains," said
one, though these, while very useful, of course, as
any woman knows, may prove more of a handicap
than a help if not cleverly concealed. But, "She
shall also have beauty," added another. Ah, that's
better, and a combination that may be both interesting and brilliant. But then, too, "She shall have
charm," pronounced a third fairy. So that was the

way they made her irresistible. Brains and beauty and charm. And the greatest of these is charm.

Besides this is her awareness of it. That is what makes all of this endowment so effectual. She knows about it, well, just as a bird knows that it has wings. You would no more expect her not to use it than you would expect a bird not to fly. Yet she is equally without vanity or any disturbing self-consciousness.

She loves beauty everywhere, in her castles, in her gardens, in her clothes. All things about her she makes beautiful. Because she lives more happily, having them so. Inspired by an artistic temperament, she has for every phase of her environment this instinctive response to beauty. How, then, can she miss it in her mirror? She doesn't. She adores it there too. And because frankness is one of her quite outstanding characteristics, she doesn't mind telling you that she likes her looks. A great many other people do, you know. And a great many of them, especially men, have told her so.

From the time that she was five, she began to hear and to learn. There was a visit to Russia that she remembers well. She and her sisters were there and a number of little royal cousins. Across the wide green lawns of a great palace, the whole flock of them came running one day. "Oh, see the pretty little one!" exclaimed a Russian uncle who singled out Missy at a glance. "And the way she has with her. Why, it's a way I'll wager will

sometime go straight to the hearts of men." Now
the uncle was a Grand Duke who knew about
women. Indeed, he achieved a continental reputa-
tion as a connoisseur in beautiful women.

The next day Missy climbed on a chair to look
at herself in a glass. She saw that she was something nice. And she never forgot, but kept the
happy idea right along in her heart. Of course
the "pretty little one" at five did not quite get all
that the Grand Duke meant. But by thirteen she
began to understand. And at twenty she had found
out all about it. To-day she cannot help but know
how successfully she can fly. But she is as imper-
sonal in estimating her values as she might be in
appraising a rare rug or a priceless vase. Easily
enough she agreed with me: "Yes, I know I am
said to be the most beautiful woman in Europe.
About that, of course, I cannot judge because I
cannot know. But about the other queens, I
know. I am the most beautiful queen in Europe.
And I am so glad to have a face that can give my
people pleasure."

"Still I have, you see," she commented meditatively, "the nose of Grandmamma the Queen."
She ran a reflective finger along the slight irregu-
larity of it that recalls the photographs of Queen
Victoria. "It is Grandmamma's nose," she repeated. "But," she added brightly, "thank God,
improved upon."

Just like that one finds her. Her grandfather,
Alexander II, was that notable Czar who freed the

serfs in Russia. Her grandmother in England was
one of the famous queens of history. Reckon, even
so, all the royalty that is descended to her. She is
all the Guelfs and all the Romanoffs, you know.
Yes, but then she is also all the Guelfs and all the
Romanoffs improved upon! For she is, you see,
herself. Brains and beauty and charm. The
greatest of these is charm. All of them together
constitute personality. And personality is power.
It's that which has made Marie of Roumania the
twentieth century's Queen of queens, though the
throne that destiny set for her was way down there
at almost the jumping off place in Europe, in a
little land that she was to make a large one.

It was up there in England that she began to be
made ready for her task. You may never forget the
influence on her life of Grandmamma the Queen.
That was a Grandmamma who lent background
not only to the household of her immediate descendants, but to the 19th century as well. All the
ladies of the generations over which she reigned,
even here in our America, followed her lead.
There were our mothers and our grandmothers
who did their hair as Victoria did. They wore
their India, or at least their Paisley, shawls and
their black silk gowns as Victoria did. In dress
and deportment, the widow at Windsor was the
model for womankind.

She became the most important person of her
age. And then, in her exalted position, something
awesome beside. I think every one came to regard

her, even as Marie, her granddaughter, says to-day in a voice hushed with gravity, as an Anglo-Saxon institution. It seemed as if she would go on forever. How would the world move without the Queen of England sitting there on the throne in Buckingham Palace, with, of course, an occasional relief by way of a visit to Windsor?

It is with the royal household at these two residences, right at the hub of the universe as one may say, that Missy's memories begin. She would have been at that time a little child with her yellow hair "banged" in front, tied back from the sides with a ribbon on top and hanging behind over her shoulders in floating wave lengths. "My picture grandchild," Queen Victoria used to call her. Her dresses, long enough to cover her knees, would have been high-necked and long-sleeved for ordinary every day. Only for parties would she have been dressed up with short sleeves and low neck and wearing a sash and gold locket and chain. Usually too, she wore high black button shoes. Slippers and white kid and yellow kid shoes were for best.

The house at Eastwell in Kent was the family's country residence. Their town house in London faced the Green Park. But both of these were just the very large houses where one lived as a matter of course and without particular interest in the environment. Much more vivid in memory even to-day are the houses of Grandmamma the Queen where one so often spent the day or the week-end.

Grandmamma the Empress was very far off. Looking backward now, there is only just a glimpse of her face worn and white with illness, the time one saw her, I think the only time. It happened to be in a railway carriage of the royal private train. It may have been a year after that Missy and Ducky with black sashes tied round their white dresses found themselves standing at a window of the Winter Palace in St. Petersburg. They were watching a funeral procession that passed by. And that was all about Grandmamma the Empress.

But Grandmamma the Queen one went to often, just as one went to church. There was a feeling that it was necessary to keep almost as still. Grandmamma seemed nearly like God. She was so good. Father always spoke of her or addressed her in a voice quite hushed and reverent as "Dearest Mamma." All the English uncles and the aunts did too.

When the grandchildren were brought to see her, Grandmamma kissed them on the forehead. They kissed her hand. It always trembled slightly. How queer and strange that was! Then she would ask, in her English voice that never had overcome its slightly German accent: Were they good children? And how were they getting on with their lessons?

One always presented, of course, as excellent a personal account as was possible about these matters. But it was never without secret apprehension lest something bad might have reached the knowledge of the awesome presence, that little old lady who sat there so still in her bunchy black silk dress and her white widow's cap.

For no matter how very tiny she was, there was about Grandmamma the Queen a sense of supreme superiority, to which no one could fail to render homage. The attitude of childhood never altered with Marie. It was when driving with Grandmamma that the little old lady seemed smaller than ever as she sat very low on her seat. A big girl beside her in the carriage seemed to tower over her, to whom she invariably commented reprovingly and a little testily: "My dear child, you sit much too high." Obediently, but in vain, the growing granddaughter tried to shrink down small.

Even when a Crown Princess, married, and in line to become a Queen on her own account, this same Marie returned for an occasional visit to England, she was invariably received at Buckingham Palace with the inquiry: "Well, my child, and what have you been doing down there?" It was what Grandmamma always called Roumania, just "down there." And the inquiry would come in a tone of voice that used to startle the present Queen of Roumania right back into little girlhood again. Had she been good? With that same old secret apprehension, she made swift survey of her conduct. Had any unfavorable report by chance reached the ears of Grandmamma the Queen?

Back from the days of childhood there echoes

yet the sound of the tap-tap-tapping along the stone corridors of the stick that Grandmamma carried when she walked. It always rested beside her chair when she sat. And there was majesty in that room. Grandmamma was not really so stern as the children thought. It was actually shyness, as much as anything else, with which she was wrapped about. But the veneration all around her made always such a worshipful quiet in her room.

A further reason also made it very solemn there. And that was the dead people. One entire corner of the room was completely occupied by those photographs which Grandmamma kept always with her, the photographs of everybody who had passed on. Of more immediate personal concern, there were the curls of dead babies' hair. It was just like the hair one had one's self. And suppose God should some day snatch one up to heaven to be with all those dead babies gone before who had left these curls behind!

These were uncomfortable reflections it was never possible to avoid. But emerging at length from the awful fascination of such reveries, one always turned for relief to the opposite corner of the room, where lived a bullfinch in a cage. Sometimes when Grandmamma was engaged in conversation and the nurse in white piqué wasn't looking, one could poke one's fingers through the cage to scare, O just ever so little you know, to scare the bullfinch.

Those nurses in white piqué, very stiff white

piqué, were always at Grandmamma's house. She kept them especially to take charge of young visitors. They took one to walk in the Green Park but never to step on the grass. Sometimes one rolled a hoop very nicely along the gravel paths. There were balloons for sale at Hyde Park corner. Very excellent conduct was rewarded by Mademoiselle with permission to buy a balloon. You could choose for yourself the color. Which should it be, with all so very beautiful? If Ducky decided for a red one, that made it simpler. Then out of all the rest Missy would have perhaps a blue one. Afterward a really perfect day would be finished off with a visit to the Soho Bazaar, where could be purchased pink rock candy. Always along with the candy came the admonition "not to break your teeth." And there was later the bother "not to soil your dress with sticky fingers."

Going regularly to see Grandmamma the Queen was the accustomed diversion of childhood. Once a year something else happened. It was the visit to the distant land where dwelt that delightful person, Grandpapa the Emperor. Strength and steadfastness of soul which are hers in marked degree, Marie in her early determining years undoubtedly drew from an Anglo-Saxon soil. But there is about her also another distinguishing characteristic, that lavishness and gayety of spirit called by the French the *joie de vivre*, joy of life. And this could have been imbibed only from a less austere source.

We were walking one day in the gardens at Sinaia and we came to the fuchsias. Do you know these flowers, once so fashionable for gardens that everybody had to have some, from Litchfield, Conn., to Charleston, S. C.? Everybody had fuchsias. And Carmen Sylva had them too at Sinaia. But, "Let's go away from these," said Marie as we hurried past them. "They make me remember such unbeautiful things, all of Grandmamma's plush furniture and the plush photograph albums with the little brass nails set in. I don't like fuchsias. Or any other mid-Victorian thing," she concluded with emphasis.

Now the place in the world that had been quite the farthest for Missy from every Victorian influence had been St. Petersburg. And it was Russia's reckless splendor that really swept her heartstrings and tuned the child for some of the high harmonies of temperament that have enriched the vivid personality of Queen Marie. On recurring special visiting occasions, the stately simplicity and the solemn awe of the customary English environment receded for a season, to give place to the pomp and pageantry that burst on one's view at the most brilliant court the world has ever seen. To Queen Victoria's little granddaughter it was like a magical awakening in the morning to find that now for a while every day would be like Christmas day.

Who in the world could compare with Grandpapa the Emperor? He and all of the Russian uncles seemed as giants belonging to a race apart.

Why, as tiny and little as was Grandmamma the Queen, so big and tall was Grandpapa the Emperor. Still there was never any mistake in the minds of the children: it was the little old lady back in Buckingham Palace who was most overwhelmingly impressive in her majesty. Despite her diminutive stature, she was never in any royal sense dwarfed by this other sovereign ancestor, delightful Grandpapa the Emperor.

But just as he was less royal, he was also less remote. And best of all, he never seemed to care so much whether you were good. He held you on his knee, and kissed your cheeks and pinched them too, and rubbed his black whiskers against your chin. And oh, how good he smelled when he smashed his face up close to yours! It was the experience of later years, of course, that disclosed the source of this perfectly delicious masculine fragrance to be a combination of Russian leather and Russian cigarettes. Missy was the favorite of Grandpapa the Emperor. She it was who always went driving with him, standing between his knees while he handled the reins over the backs of his swiftest trotters. He insisted on driving himself. At the Tsarskoe Selo Palace all of the children had their measles. Missy was the last to come down with them, and it was on the edge of her bed that Grandpapa sat to tell them stories.

That was the last visit to Grandpapa the Emperor. They had been home in England only a little while after the measles, when one day their mother was crying. She was crying not with just a few little tears. She was crying with a very terrible sobbing that did not stop. And she told them that God had taken Grandpapa the Emperor.

That was what she said, that God had taken him. But the servants told them something else. Mademoiselle, the nursery governess, said it was the Nihilists. Anyhow, Czar Alexander II had been removed by a bomb. And Alexander III, their mother's brother, now reigned in his stead over 140 million subjects.

You see how it is: that ruling has always been, as one may say, a very customary occupation for her family. And now one may understand what she means about Ion, the potter's son. It was near Sinaia in a village on the mountain side that Ion lived. And we went one day to have him make some bowls for which we brought the pattern. Mashka carried one bowl and I the other. With every lurch of the automobile the Queen cautioned us to be careful. The bowls were very precious because she had unearthed them from old ruins in the Island of Malta. Their lines were so lovely, and she had known at once that she must have bowls like these for flowers at Castle Bran. So we brought them to Ion. Could he reproduce them?

Ion sat there, a boy before his potter's wheel: black hair, black eyes, heavy black eyebrows, long curling black eyelashes. He wore homespun white wool trousers and a white tunic fastened with a Roman striped red belt about his waist. Over the bowl that the Queen handed him he passed swift feeling fingers, until he seemed to sense its shape. He reached for the wet clay. With a touch from his bare foot, he started the belt that sent his wheel awhirling. Against it he held the ball of clay, modeling the material now this way, now that, with frequent glances at the pattern before him. In ten minutes, he had ready one bowl. In another ten minutes, the second stood beside it. Each had been produced with such perfection that they could not be told from those originals of centuries before.

One marvels at such skill. But you see Ion makes all the pitchers and pots and bowls for this village. His father before him and all his grandfathers were potters. So that the skill to make pitchers and pots and bowls is now in Ion an inherited instinct. It is the customary occupation for his family to be potters.

The Queen pointed out as we went away how one peasant makes pitchers and bowls, another shoes, another cart wheels. Each does what his ancestors did before him, because it's in his blood to do that particular job better than it can be done by anyone else. "That's how I have my inheritance too," she concluded. "Just so I was born to the business of ruling."

Now the land where she was to do this ruling had been a long while making ready for her. Some 1800 years before her arrival, Emperor Trajan conquering Decebel, the King of Dacia, set the first boundaries here of a colony that was called

Romania. And Roman in thought and feeling it was to remain right down through the ages. Successive invasions of barbarians rolled over it, the Goths, the Huns, the Avars. Then came the Turks. And the country that was to be hers was for a thousand years obscured in the darkness of their oriental despotism. Surrounding empires also every little while took their toll of territory; Austria got the Bucovina, Hungary acquired Transylvania, and Russia annexed Bessarabia. In the struggle for national survival, there stand out two great leaders of the former free Principalities, Stefan the Great of Moldavia and Mihai the Brave of Wallachia. With the reverberation of the French revolution round the world, the common people here in Roumania also had begun to find themselves. Arising against the native nobility, the Boyars in 1854 freed the serfs and abolished feudalism.

Relief from Turkish oppression came at last with the intervention finally of the seven great powers constituting the Congress of Paris. The first Roumanian parliament for the United Principalities assembled in 1861. It was decided to invite a member of a foreign royal family to accept Roumanian nationality and rulership. So Carol of the Sigmaringen branch of the House of Hohenzollern arrived from Germany to become the Prince of Roumania, still subject, however, in some measure to the Sublime Porte. This German Prince it was who led the Roumanian army to the aid of the Russians in that battle of Plevna which in 1877 defeated the Turks and completely freed the country which had so long suffered under their tyranny. In 1881 Carol was crowned King, thus establishing for this very old land a very new dynasty.

To his wife, Elizabeth of Wied, was born only one child, a little daughter who died at four years of age. So there was adopted to succeed King Carol, his brother's son, Ferdinand. And while a little English princess was growing up to become the wife of this young man, the old King was organizing and setting in order the kingdom she was later to adorn. The army that had been assembled was diligently trained. Government departments were set up, public buildings erected and industries and banks established. The constitution of a limited monarchy had been adopted. And all titles had been abolished. Out of the mists of medievalism a modern kingdom was to arise, the foundations of which were being laid with German thoroughness.

Now this country, which the granddaughter of Queen Victoria was destined to lead through the intricate pages of twentieth century history, lies away over on the far side of civilization. It is the last land in Europe. The Black Sea washes its shores. Beyond lies Asia.

Yet out of a Roumania over which the centuries have rolled there is arising to-day a modern kingdom. And the significant fact is that everywhere you look there is apparent the touch of a woman's hand that is making this old world new.

That a woman should have made Greater Roumania great is probably the strangest thing that could have come to pass in a country so east from everywhere else. You see the lady is not in law the ruler of Roumania. Her husband is. As the consort of Ferdinand I, who is King, she need never have done aught else than sit on the throne beside him. Nobody expected her to. But you remember how she was born, the blood of her fathers that's in her veins, and the beauty that's in her face. By what a narrow chance all the history that she has made might have been missed! Not far from this land, they veil the women in Turkey. In Roumania by good luck the *marama* has always been worn thrown *back* from the face. Women here may be seen, but not heard. The silence is particularly enforced from the precepts of St. Paul. Fortunately though, one notes, even he said nothing at all about charm.

And oh, the charm of her! The charm of her! Seemingly there is nothing at all that she does. She simply is. It happens as naturally as a flower exudes fragrance. Such is the charm that radiates from her presence. It is as inevitable that men should come to follow it as that bees should seek a flower.

There are moments when this charm sparkles in the glance of her blue eyes. But see, now she has dropped the white lids. And the same magic is in the soft little smile that has slid down the rounded tea rose cheeks to play about the corners of a very pretty mouth. But the glance from the blue eyes that dropped the smile that plays so fascinatingly about the pretty mouth somehow was loaded. It has discharged a dart that arrived straight at its destination, which is the heart of the nearest man. And it matters not whether that man be peasant or courtier. Something has exhilarated him like champagne. You should see the marvelous dahlias that Conrad raises; Conrad, the German gardener. Because he does it for Her.

There was an army division encamped near Castle Bran for their summer maneuvers. The officers were asked for tea one day in the garden. The gardens at Bran lie at the base of the high rock on which the castle stands. A cluster of them circle round it. This was the old-fashioned garden, where the apple tree stands and the hollyhocks grow and marigolds and lavender and lupin and verbena and love-in-a-mist. There are wandering paths and a brook tinkles through. It was under a larch tree the tea table was set with all sorts of sandwiches and cakes that day. After the feasting, the moment came when the men stood in two long lines with a grassy lane between. The Queen stepped down it to the strains of the "Traiasca" the band began to play. She had selected for the day her most gorgeous embroideries. She wore her red slippers. She had clasped about her waist a massive belt of silver and turquoises. It may in the long ago have belonged to a Dacian chieftain. In the belt hung the Scandinavian dagger she always wears with her native costume. But beneath all this barbaric splendor, there was still the eternal feminine.

And two lines of soldiers thrilled to it. As she stepped off, every man's hand went to his head in salute. She stopped before each and gave him her hand to kiss. And she decorated him with a dahlia for his buttonhole. In every man's face was worship and reverence and wonder at her. I watched their eyes. Those beautiful dark Roumanian eyes all followed her as if a magnet drew them. The devotion they offered Her Majesty was as to a goddess divine though what each in his heart was repeating, one felt, was "My Queen." And the band played softly the sweet wild strains of the "Traiasca."

"That," she said to me afterwards, "is what I call a good day's work for the King. It is when you have the army with you that King and country are safe."

There were statesmen too on whom the witchery of her charm was worked while I watched it. Two came to Bran whose names you know through the newspaper cables.

One was Roumanian and one was French. In the garden the statesmen too drank their tea. And the blue-eyed glance of the Queen played alternately and impartially over each. It was exactly as if a sunbeam shone now this way, now that.

63

And so cleverly she flashed from one to the other, that each felt always he had the lady's particular attention. Now one was bald and the other gray-headed. But in the effulgence of the royal presence that summer afternoon both elderly gentlemen bloomed out like boys again. They got their dahlias too. "But Your Majesty is the fairest flower of all," murmured the Frenchman above the hand he kissed at his coat lapel. They stayed until the gold green light that precedes the dusk was framing the turrets of Castle Bran. Then they rode away in their motor car some twenty years young. And statecraft had been done that day. I don't know what it was she filled their minds with while she turned their heads because she was doing it all in French. But whatever the events she sent them about, it was perfectly apparent how happy they were to serve, how delighted to oblige. What wouldn't they do for Her? Such is the diplomacy in the smile of this woman as it warms the hearts of men.

It's Nicky, her son, who knows about this. He is, to be sure, Prince Nicolai. But from the moment you meet him, he comes to be the kind of a boy who'd got to have the short and affectionate name. You can start to laugh when Nicky begins to talk, because you will always have to. I heard Nicky epitomize for his mother one day her influence on a visiting diplomat. "I tell you, Ma'am," he finished, "the man just can't keep his eyes in

64

his head while you're around. Has to take 'em out and put 'em in his pocket."

At Constanza, which is Roumania's seaport city, waited the English battle cruiser *Frobisher,* on which Nicky was leaving to rejoin his ship. He's in the English navy now, you know, learning seamanship. The royal train took Her Majesty from Sinaia to the recently built new palace at Constanza: there on the eve of Nicky's departure she gave a supper to which were invited the English staff officers with Roumanian officers to meet them. "Oh, mother," whispered radiant Nicky, "the effect of your smile to-night will never come off. It's going to last for all my life. What was I before but an unknown little lieutenant! Now every man here will always see you in me. I'm no more just myself for them. I'm the son of the Queen of Roumania."

"I was glad, of course, the boy was pleased," the Queen explained to me. "But there was more than Nicky in my purpose. It was the *bonne entente* between two nations I was cementing that night through their navy."

The *bonne entente,* or the *entente cordiale!* Ah, and who so adept as Marie at taking the strain from situations personal or political? But the skill that now put states at peace was really first acquired right in the limited sphere most anciently assigned her sex. Some of her most useful discoveries were made in the domestic circle. One day she announced as a theorem: "Ferdinand, there is no one in the world I could not put on cordial terms with anyone else."

"But that is impossible," rejoined the King. "Me, for example. You could never make me feel that way for some one I disliked."

"Yes, Ferdinand, even you. I've done it," she insisted. And now the King was almost angry. His wife was smiling. And there was nothing funny that he could see. But also he began to be curious. "Well, how then?' he demanded.

"Like this, my dear," she said. "You know how you used to detest the Duchess of X——? Maybe you remember, too, the time I came and told you how the Duchess of X—— nevertheless thought you the handsomest man and the cleverest man she knew.

"And that began to interest you. You asked next day for just the words she said it in. The real words, of course, I couldn't recall. But the next time you met the Duchess of X—— you looked at the lady as at one whom you had never before really seen. Fine woman that, after all. She had suddenly become an individual of such excellent taste. Such a comfortable joyous feeling spread over you as relaxed your soul. And never again, from that day to this, have you had to have the stomach ache at the thought of the Duchess of X——. She had been, you see, utterly transformed. To-day, my dear, I notice you find the Duchess of X—— one of the most charming women of your acquaintance."

Well, a long while after, the King laughed.

Now Ferdinand I of Roumania is naturally just like any husband. Then, being German beside—— And you've heard how everywhere east of the Rhine the supremacy of man must be maintained. It often seems wisest that a woman go softly and a long way around to get what she wants when she wants it. See how some years ago, the Queen got Nicky first sent to Eton.

In the course of his growing up, it had come time for this second son of the family to go away to school. And the Queen had quite made up her mind just where she meant him to go. There remained the King's mind to be made up. Do you suppose she said Eton to the boy's father? She said it instead to a General, a warrior whose opinion would be so much weightier than a wife's. Would the General care to have tea with her one day? And while he drank the tea, she filled him full of Eton and the greatness of all who had been graduated there. A little later, the King in search of advice about schooling for his son, got it. The General knew, because he had been so very well told, that Eton would be exactly the place. And then the King knew too. In due course of time came the announcement: "My dear, Nicky must go to Eton. It's a far country, I know. And of course you won't want him to go. But I've decided. There's just one place for the boy. And it's Eton. Now don't say a word, my dear."

She didn't. Not that kind of word. The

mother of Nicky just looked very carefully down at her dinner plate: "Well, of course, Ferdinand, you know best."

These I have cited are but instances presented by way of illustration. Wouldn't it have been a pity to limit the application of skill like this? Domesticity develops such excellent technique in the management of men. But for the hearthside or for halls of government the same tactics are admirably and equally adapted. This lady had only to extend her method. It has availed as magically in national affairs. Aye, in international too. The Queen stated it to me almost as an axiom: "I always do my work through others. Sometimes it must be a long while and a long way around. But eventually that which I have planned comes to pass." Just like that, she said it. Woman's rights! Votes for women! Here's a woman doesn't need such slapdash stuff. Votes by men will do. When she decides them.

As I have pointed out, Marie of Roumania need never have bothered her head with any government matter. Nobody expected her to. Yet even with the eastern way they have things fixed for women down there, it had to come to pass. Little by little the sphere of her influence widened. A bird that has wings would be bound to fly. The blood of her fathers she had in her veins, you know—and that of her grandmother too. To-day so much in reality a sovereign in her husband's country has she become that the Queen of Roumania is the best known royalty in the world.

And she sits enthroned in majesty in days like these when so much royalty is diminishing in the distance down the stage of time—and some of it stepping off backwards with a smash. Ruler after ruler around her has gone to the discard. Three empires have crumbled across her very boundary lines. But even as other monarchs have decreased, she has increased. As they have made their exits, she has made her entrance to take the center of a stage that seems to have been set for her.

A ruler, Marie of Roumania has told me, is born, not made. In that golden room again I hear the steady even tones that are reading her life to me. O, her belief in her right to rule is well enough founded. Brains and beauty and charm. Yes, God made her so.

Nor is her Roumania the only land she could have ruled. On her way to this, her skirts brush by another throne. A gentleman who sits thereon to-day remembers well. In days gone by a girl there was that he held dear. But along the curving path of fate, she whirled away, on careless eager feet dancing to destiny. How he remembers! Now and again across the years he looks, and across the continent of Europe. And he remembers and remembers and cannot forget.

The gentleman is George the Fifth, the present King of England. Missy! Oh, Missy!

She is so very royal.

69

CHAPTER III

Her Garden of Dreams

MYSTERIOUS, mystical, magical, you know a crystal has always been. The Queen has one. It stands on her boudoir dressing table, a lovely silvery sphere of glass. And when a chance sunbeam now and then sets it all aflame, it glows with fiery color. This talisman Her Majesty keeps ever near her. When she travels, it is the first article packed by her maid. It goes always with her. For it is useful, you see, a desk clock; a dial is cleverly set inside of the crystal, by which to tell time. And it has ticked off for Marie of Roumania all the years of her life since the time that comes once to us all when the earth shines out with a great glory that afterward is gone.

Thereby hangs the real tale of the crystal. Would you guess it? The rainbow of her youth is imprisoned there. And the lady has only to gaze deeply and everything comes true again. She sees once more the soft green look of spring. She hears the call of the birds. She feels again the splendor of sunlit days and the opal poignancy of moonlight and the velvety touch of the dark green night in the wind that brushes her cheek. Oh, all the wonder of the world, the beautiful wonderful world that was before the whole scene faded and its lovely colors dripped away in the drab day-after-day reality of life, all this is with her again. The crystal, you see, has the power to bring back everything that ever was. Around the glass ball is a golden band traced with fine lettering. The Queen, quietly smiling, passed it to me to read: "From George to Darling Missy Christmas 1891," it says. Of course, I looked back with a question in my eyes. The Queen nodded. And then she told me all about Malta.

On this island in the Mediterranean were spent the happiest years of her childhood. Her father, the Duke of Edinburgh, was the Admiral at the British naval station there. The family residence was a spacious old palace. It was set in the most beautiful yellow-walled gardens with quaint arching doorways that give passage from one to the other. And the rarest of flowers grew in those gardens. The Queen says: "Sometimes I catch their fragrance yet, a crushing delicious sweetness. But I seem to smell them like fairy flowers I shall never see again."

Malta was made for romance. Standing in the sea between Sicily and Africa, it shimmers always in the yellow light of a southern sun. High above it hangs a heaven that is an azure canopy, the brilliance of which shades and softens into rose and pink and purple, and through these sunset streams, liquid orange and gold and crimson. It is a far-flung splendor that no horizon hems. For whatever color the sky carries, all the sea is washed with it too in a mirrored reflection that makes the Mediterranean itself like another flowing firmament of color. Bathed in this beauty, the gray island has lifted its rocky area of some hundred square miles since the most ancient of days. Prehistoric temples, still standing on its shores, have echoed with the earliest petitions of man to God. One civilization after another has lived and loved here and folded away its record of laughter and tears. Phœnicians and Romans, Greeks and Carthaginians, Saracens and Normans, all of them passed this way. The red-painted two-wheeled carts the natives still use in the high steep streets are reminiscent of those that Hannibal rode in. And the bright, painted boats that rock in every inlet might have been stepped out of yesterday by Cæsar's legions. It was on this island that St. Paul was shipwrecked and the church that he founded still keeps alive the altar fires of early Christian tradition. Valetta, the main city, was built by the Knights of St. John, who made it the shield of Christendom when this was their stronghold, where the cross defeated the crescent in the struggle between Christians and Turk. It is the city of their magnificent palaces still preserved here and filled with their precious treasures of the past ages. Into this heritage in 1800 entered the British, whose great fortified stronghold on the route to the east Malta is to-day.

And out of the northland, in the eighties, came here in her tenth year the little English princess whose girlhood playground the ancient island was to be. It was the land of sunshine that particularly invited her bright and sunny spirit. Some four miles out of Valetta, the old Palace of San Antonio, built in 1625 by the Grand Master of the Knights, Anthony de Paula, had been long used as the summer residence for the governor of the island. It was now set aside for the occupancy of the Duke of Edinburgh. His connection with the fleet had several times before brought the family here for short sojourn. So it had happened that Ducky, the second sister, had been born here; it was for this they had christened her Victoria Melita, which is the ancient spelling for Malta. Now the family had come to make their permanent home here for some four years.

What they were like, the little girls who found their carefree childish happiness here, the Queen summed up for me. "I was gay, sunny, frivolous, not learning my lessons very easily, but loving everybody. Ducky, a year younger but looking older, was my inseparable companion. Sandra, three years younger than I, was different, quite different from both of us, slower, more practical, less imaginative. Baby B was the spoiled darling of the family and very naughty. Of us all, I was the show sister. I was a little girl very good to look upon. I can say it unblushingly, because it was so."

73

One great advantage there was at Malta, which was a distinct contribution in character formation for the little Princess who was later to be a Queen: here life was lived much less formally and ceremoniously than would have been possible at any European court. The little girls were allowed to relax from royalty and to be themselves, just happy little human beings. They were dressed always very plainly and all three alike. For play they were put into gray Holland linen pinafores. And if a pinafore was torn, it was not replaced with a new one; instead, it was carefully darned.

Outside the walls of San Antonio nearby lived the superintendent of parks for Valetta; he had two little daughters, Lily and Angelina, to whom it was a great comfort to notice the darns in the royal pinafores. And it helped undoubtedly to establish the undercurrent of comradeship in the salutations exchanged when the Princesses passed by. It was Missy who never failed to call out, "Hello, Lily!" "Hello, Angelina!" in that same democracy of spirit which is to-day a distinguishing trait of the Queen of Roumania. Not all the majesty that makes her a sovereign has ever been able to hedge her away from any interesting contact that life has offered.

It was the lovely gardens of San Antonio that were the Princesses' playground. These gardens opened one from the other in long-drawn-out mystery, each presenting ever a fresh picture of enchantment to Missy and Ducky, as hand in hand they jumped the low stone thresholds. It was among the rarest of flowers and foliage that they romped and roamed. Dark Norfolk Island pines towered among giant English oak trees. Orange trees and lemon trees beneath cool waxen leaves hung out lantern globes of golden color. Pepper trees waved like green lace in the wind. Oleander trees bloomed in overpowering sweet pinkness. Clambering roses made of sunflecked pergolas scented bowers of beauty. Geraniums, pink and red, draped the garden walls in riotous profusion. Long lines of garden path were phalanxed by stately calla lilies standing in green and white line. Wide basins here and there brimmed with water lilies, opening yellow honeyed hearts. Poinsettias and hybiscus waved their flaming flowers like flags. Carefully laid-out beds were filled with choice plants, which the gardeners by the constant procession of change kept ever blooming in synchrony with the passing seasons. And everything that grew gave out its distilled sweetness on the tropical air, mingling in the haunting fragrance that Missy would never forget. Fountains of silvery falling water tinkled musically among the flowers. Greek marbles from this very old part of the world lent the marvel of their line and coloring to the scene.

"All this loveliness was mine," says the Queen of Roumania with a reminiscent thrill in her voice to-day, "when life lay before me like a beautiful story. And Ducky and I were there together."

Hear how the Queen says that. It is ever with caressing affection that she mentions the name of this favorite sister. In the golden room at the castle at Sinaia, where we talked through the midnight hours, I noticed the pictured face the Queen keeps nearest her. On the golden wall above her divan hangs a portrait from which look out the mystical Russian eyes of the sister whom she has ever cherished in a love that memorably links these two. Always it has been joy enough just that they might be together. And in those days of their little girlhood, happiness was quite complete.

Their education proceeded in the great square schoolroom with a stone floor in a wing of the palace under the direction of a German governess. And there were outside teachers who came daily for special subjects. French seemed a great joke to Missy and Ducky, that silly language much affected by grown-ups. They always nudged each other and laughed together when they heard their elders use it. For themselves, they quite avoided it except at compulsory recitation periods.

The music mistress was Miss Mary Butler, who came out twice a week from Valetta in a horse-drawn *carrozin,* as the little carriages, black curtained and upholstered in white linen, are called. She was dressed in mustard-colored plush and a wonderful hat with pink ostrich feathers. And there always lingered about her that nice smell of kid gloves. Where, by the way, has that wonderful odor gone? Kid gloves no longer have it.

But they certainly had it in those days, as any one who remembers the eighties may distinctly recall. Miss Mary Butler used to go on from San Antonio to another palace even 300 years older, where she taught music also to the little Baroness Mary D'Amico Inguanez, who belonged to the oldest nobility on the island. It was Missy who used frequently to inquire of Miss Butler, "Was the Baroness Mary ever bad?" Because she herself, as everybody knew, gave the music mistress no little trouble over her "notes." Still, Miss Butler always reported to her mother that Missy, though wayward, was a most winsome child.

For long bright hours after lessons were done the children were as free as the butterflies to flit about the garden. Tony, the policeman who guarded the palace grounds, always kept a watchful eye on them. They spent much of their time following closely at the heels of George, the head gardener. The Queen of Roumania is to-day a specialist in flowers because she learned it from him. To each child he allotted seeds and plants and garden space which, under his direction and with a miniature set of garden tools, were carefully cultivated.

George was so useful in other ways, too. Often he left his stepladder standing conveniently against a tree. Or even he could occasionally be persuaded to give a boost straight from his shoulder. And a start like that was all one needed. "They climb like squirrels," he used to tell Tony. Each

77

child had her own particular tree. And Missy's was the tallest, the dark Norfolk Island pine that stands 85 feet high. "She'd skin straight to the top of it," the old gardener will tell you reminiscently if you go down there to Malta to-day. "And somersaults, why bless you, those children, any of 'em, 'ud roll along a garden path like a ball."

For playmates they had three little girl companions, Mab and Elsa and Ina, the daughters of a friend of their mother, who visited much at San Antonio. And these were always the "monkeys" for the tree-climbing game in which Missy and her sisters were the "masters." There were the dogs to romp with; Sandy, a brown spaniel; Tostik, a black Russian dog; and Snowball, a little white Maltese. But it was their horses the children loved best; Ruby, the beautiful Arabian that belonged to Missy; Fearless, who was Ducky's, and Tommy, who was Sandra's.

Just like all other and less royal children, these little girls liked to play at the game of being a grown-up. They had what was called the "dressing-up basket," to which from time to time the Duchess, their mother, made contributions of gowns and hats. And if ever the dressing-up basket ran low, ah well, never mind, a table cloth might be fashioned into a court train and a crown could always be cut from gilt paper. The crown was very necessary. Missy it was who wore it.

And all the games began with her announcement, "Now, I am going to be a queen."

It was great luck one day when they found an old cupboard which had been discarded from somewhere in the household. Their mother said, yes, they might have it. Missy and Ducky set industriously to work and decorated it outside and in with pictures while Sandra passed the brushes and the paint. It was a lovely house when it was done. Then the children looked at each other: What was the house for? Why, for a husband and wife to live in. "Well, then," announced Ducky to Missy, "I'll have to be the husband and you shall be my wife and Sandra shall be the servant. I'll just have to be the husband to take care of you."

And that would do very nicely. A husband who should take care of her, that was what Missy looked forward to. He must be big and strong and handsome, but especially big and strong, a man whom she could look up to, who could take care of her and to whom she could be a faithful, loving wife. That was going to be a large order for some one some day. It would have to be a great man who could match up as the required soul mate. For this girl, now on the threshold of life, was going to be a great woman.

The children grew older. And now there was a new interest. There began to be boys. And there was a whole English fleet of them, young midshipmen in their teens. Parties were given at the San Antonio palace, with dancing and Blindman's Buff in the winter. In the summer the young midshipmen came to tea in the gardens and "Follow your Leader" was played with a free range throughout all the palace from the store rooms and the kitchens on the ground floor even up to the flat-topped Italian roof. And the boys gave parties in return on their ships, "cookie" parties was what they called them. Saturday there was always a picnic, when the Duchess organized a party of young people to spend the day on the beach. Along narrow high-walled roads, through tight-walled little villages they went, past lovely old yellow houses with blinds and doors of green or pink or blue or lavender. St. Paul's Bay, about a five-mile ride, was a favorite destination. The Duchess and Baby B came in the carriage. The servants followed with lunch on the red-wheeled cart, called a *carratun*. The girls, on their ponies, with their escorts rode ahead. Each had her own special midshipman. To Missy belonged one David Beatty.

To-day all the world knows him as the famous Admiral Beatty. He came a few years since on some English government mission to Roumania. A great dinner was given in his honor at the royal palace in Bucharest. He sat next the Queen. At first she was formally Your Majesty. But after a while the Admiral said, "Missy, I find you still as vibrantly interested in life as when we ate cookies together in Malta." He added, "There's something I wonder if you've forgotten." From his vest pocket he took out a quite curious little object, which he laid on the table between their two gold plates. The Queen's eyes opened in amused surprise and then brimmed blue with laughter: "My parting gift to you, my Malta midshipman," she exclaimed. "You promised to remember me by it always."

"So I have," submitted the Admiral. "It's been the talisman that's brought all the good luck of my career," and he put the little bronze mouse back in the pocket next his heart, "where I've carried it, Missy," he said, "for more than thirty years."

Now, in those Malta days David was nice to have always around for parties and picnics. But there was some one of much more importance, who was more of a real grown-up young man. He was Cousin George, who was nine years older than Missy. A sub-lieutenant on his uncle's ship, he spent many of his week-ends at the San Antonio palace. Among the children Missy was his favorite. Always it was she who sat on the seat beside him in the carriage when the family rode out to view the sunset. And Missy, you know, was getting to be now more than ten.

She was thirteen before anybody guessed what would happen. Then a significant incident occurred. On a summer's day the three girls on their ponies were accompanying their mother and a friend of hers for a day's outing. They had come to a steep mountain declivity where it was necessary for the Duchess and Lady Ellen to leave their carriage and everybody was to proceed on foot. "But," said the Duchess, "Lady Ellen is delicate and I want her to have one of your ponies."

Now there was instant mutinous rebellion. For Lady Ellen the children held an especial dislike, which had been carefully fostered by a governess who held a grudge against her. Simultaneously Missy and Ducky and Sandra shook their heads. "She's too big," declared Missy. "She'd break a pony's legs."

Well, of course, the Duchess silenced such outrageous frankness. The Lady Ellen got a pony, Missy's beloved Ruby. But the children got their revenge. It was Ducky who thought it up. On the return trip, the Duchess and her friend had resumed their carriage and the children were again on their ponies. Suddenly, at a signal from Ducky, all three galloped furiously past the carriage, each with her tongue stuck out mockingly at Lady Ellen.

Mortification and misery of course overwhelmed their humiliated mother. "Bad, unchristian spirit," she told them, when they had reached home. "They'd have to ask God to forgive them. For no one else could."

They were sent to bed without supper and sentenced to stay in the schoolroom for a week. Meantime their horses must stand in the stable. Ah, that was terrible! For by that token all of their midshipmen friends would learn of their disgrace. They were suffering through the second day of their trouble when Cousin George arrived. He came straight to the schoolroom: "What's it all about?" he wanted to know.

And Missy flung herself in his arms to sob out the whole story. Perhaps the young man held her longer than was quite necessary for consolation. He kissed her and dried her tears with his handkerchief. He laughed and said it was all a mistake and there was no wickedness at all about what they had done, which was a great relief to all three, to hear they were not so bad they'd have to be some day barred from heaven. Afterward Ducky had drawn a lovely picture of the three with their tongues sticking out as they rode past the lady in the carriage.

Now the whole incident of the kiss might perhaps have been casual. But it wasn't something finished. It was something only begun. Both George and Missy now found themselves looking at each other with a strange new shyness. Missy didn't care so much any more to play "Follow your Leader." Ducky complained of her dreaming.

The next thing that happened, Missy was fourteen. There was going to be a family celebration for which Cousin George was coming. And she was dressed for the occasion. She was still a flat little girl with golden hair hanging down her back. But she had on a white dress with a bustle, which in those days of the eighties was quite like a young lady. And about her throat was a coral necklace.

She was in the drawing-room when George came in. It happened that no one else was there. "I say, Missy," he exclaimed. "My word, but you are pretty." And suddenly he had caught her in his arms and kissed her. This time there was no mistaking. There was nothing cousinly in it at all. This way Missy had never been kissed before. Her blue eyes in their divine astonishment opened in a new wide wonder. There were more kisses to follow. For it was first love that had occurred to both boy and girl. And soon their elders began to notice it.

Now of course, in those days of their youth, no one so much as supposed that George of England would ever be able to offer Missy a crown. It was only later, by the accident of the death of his elder brother, that the present King of England came to his throne. But when he was a naval lieutenant and Missy wore a bustle he was merely the Duke of York and only a younger son. And matters of place like that must be carefully reckoned with in royal love affairs. Even so, Queen Victoria was rather pleased than otherwise. Missy's father would have approved. But Missy's mother it was who declared the match impossible and proceeded to make it so. Right away George found himself no longer invited so often for week-ends at the San Antonio palace.

Marie Alexandrovna herself, you see, had married a second son. A haughty Russian Grand Duchess, the daughter of an Emperor, she arrived in England to find that she must give precedence at court to others, even to her husband's sisters. Her most beautiful daughter, she determined, should not repeat that experience. For Missy she had high ambitions. And to their fulfillment approaching events now contributed.

Missy was nearly fifteen when the Duke of Edinburgh's command in Malta came to an end. He had inherited the title and estate of his uncle, the Duke of Saxe Coburg and Gotha. So it was decided that at Coburg, in Germany, the family should now take up their residence. It would not be so far from Davenport, Plymouth, where the Duke's duties as Lord High Admiral would now from time to time require his presence. In April, when Malta was loveliest, the time for departure came. And George would be leaving now for England. In the garden at San Antonio he and Missy said good-by, in the garden heavy with the scent of flowers so fairly sweet that neither will ever find such fragrance again. The blue heaven in Missy's eyes was divine, indeed, that night.

The Admiral and his family sailed away in his flagship, the *Minotaur*. The flags waved. The guns saluted. The band played "God Save the Queen." And Missy and Ducky and Sandra wept unrestrainedly. Their mother said they bawled. They did not want to go to Germany. Nor did they like it any better after they arrived there. They were all put into heavy German linen underwear instead of their customary finest batiste. There was a green dress with a yellow check that Missy had to wear for a year. And now all of the girls were getting that training in housewifery which in Germany may no more than French or music be omitted from the educational curriculum of even a royal princess. In a specially arranged little outdoor pavilion all summer there were cooking lessons. Missy and Ducky and Sandra themselves prepared all of the vegetables; even they dug their own potatoes, and that they considered real fun.

But now they hurried her growing up. Missy was a wild little girl who didn't want to get to be a lady too soon. Her dresses had to be lengthened in spite of her protests. She and Ducky were confirmed at the Lutheran church in Coburg. There were Russian and German princes now who began coming this way to visit. Missy rather liked the handsome ones. But the Duchess easily nipped their intentions. "Didn't Missy know," she said to her daughter, "that these men who seemed so charming were kissing also the maids behind the parlor door!"

Even a seemingly quite eligible Russian Grand Duke George who came with a request for Missy's hand in marriage the Duchess turned away. And she quietly confiscated the gifts he afterwards sent in pressing his suit. All this, Missy herself did not hear of until later years. But the courts of Europe were buzzing with the rumor. George, now in England, heard it with alarm. Ill with

typhoid and unable to write himself, he induced
his sister to take the letter at his dictation. Missy,
Missy, what could it mean? he asked. He was
hearing of another George who was playing about
at Coburg. And he couldn't bear it. Wasn't it
all understood? He had supposed that Missy belonged to him and that some day, of course, they
would be married.

Well, the Duchess saw the letter. It was under
maternal pressure that Missy wrote her reply. In
a very grown-up way she pointed out that there
had been nothing definite in their arrangements.
They were just cousins, after all. And that was
all they ever could be.

It was some time after this letter that the crystal
Christmas present came. And then first love was
finally swept aside by the rush of events arranged
by a determined, match-making mother. But it
has never been forgotten. The King of England
on his throne looks across a continent to-day and
remembers. And the Queen of Roumania turns
her magical crystal in her white hand and smiles
reminiscently. A few years since, in the course of
international affairs, there was a state dinner at
Buckingham Palace in London. After dinner
conversation among the guests had waxed in-
formal. The modern young woman's style in dress
was under discussion. Princess Mary's short skirts
did not meet with her father's approval. "The
girl I have always liked best," said the King reminiscently, "is the girl with the bustle." And the

King of England looked across the room. But it was not at the Queen of England. It was the eyes of the Queen of Roumania that his eyes sought.

CHAPTER IV

And So They Married Her

ONE of the most fundamental precepts of the courts of Europe is that it is wisest to marry off princesses young. Otherwise they may develop ideas of their own and it may not be done at all.

The Duchess of course was looking around. And in that she was ably assisted by a very intimate friend of hers who spent much time at Coburg, the Princess Charlotte of Prussia, sister of the Emperor of Germany. Charlotte liked travel. She went about much among the courts of Europe. And she rather prided herself, as the saying went, on always "having a king or so in her pocket." It was from one of these journeys that Charlotte returned with news of importance for her friend the Duchess. There was, she announced, a perfectly good throne waiting down in Roumania and an heir apparent in search of a wife. A princess well connected with leading royal houses was what was wanted.

Down there in Roumania too a first love affair had just been successfully smudged out. Ferdinand, the Crown Prince, had been even publicly engaged to a lady-in-waiting. But there was intervention on the part of Emperor Wilhelm of Germany. A decree by King Carol had at last forbidden the marriage as not royal enough for a Hohenzollern or for the new dynasty which they had set up in this southern land. Ferdinand of Roumania must make an alliance more in keeping with his kingly prospects. Down there they were now busily engaged in tabulating all the princesses of Europe. Soon the royal heir, as Charlotte announced, would be sent north with his list in hand to look them over.

This was most valuable information, on which the Duchess did not fail to act. Missy, and Ducky with her, was called from the schoolroom. There would be no waiting for any formal coming out. Preparations were made for their immediate presentation at the German court. Missy was not yet out of her fifteenth year and Ducky was fourteen when they were taken on a visit to Wilhelmshöhe to be presented to Kaiser Wilhelm and his wife. Young as they were, they attended all of the state dinners. A year later there was another trip. They were going first to Munich, the Duchess announced. And it was in Munich, and seemingly quite by accident so far as Missy knew, that they met the young Roumanian Crown Prince Ferdinand.

The Prince carried in his vest pocket that list of eligible young ladies carefully compiled by King Carol and the Roumanian court. Among the names there was one that was specially starred.

It was that of Marie, the Princess of Edinburgh. On arrival in Germany, the young man had conferred also with his supreme relative, the Kaiser, who had enthusiastically endorsed the same selection. In America we have a saying that "she's a peach of a girl." Similarly and yet a little differently they say it beyond the Rhine. "She's the top of the basket," unequivocally affirmed the Kaiser. For that, might not a young man forget even the forbidden fruit of first love they had taken from him in his native land!

At any rate, the Prince on his own account, at his first glimpse of the fair little northern princess, was not slow to discover her charm. Her surpassing loveliness left no chance at all for any other candidate for his heart and his title. No need to look farther. This blue-eyed, golden girl would be the Queen he wanted. Could he get her? For the shy, boyish Prince courtship seemed a difficult undertaking to contemplate. But in reality he had no cause for anxiety. Everybody was going to help. Missy's destiny was already as clearly defined as if it had been completed.

Then came the evening on which Ferdinand was presented by the Duchess to her young daughter. He brought a bouquet of roses. And the two young people all the evening sat apart in the hotel bay window. There was little conversation. They mostly looked at the moon, with occasional surreptitious glances at each other.

Next the Duchess and her daughter went again

to visit the Kaiser at the New Palace in Potsdam. A little later it happened that the young Roumanian Prince came too. Her mother took occasion often to speak to Missy about his prospects in life. He was ten years older than she. Some day he would be a king. And that meant of course a throne for the fortunate girl who should get him for a husband. The entire German court, too, seemed to talk of nothing else but the eligibility of this young man who everybody now knew had been sent to make a marriage survey. Even Missy at last could not miss the meaning of what everybody was saying. Oh, diplomats, courtiers, and kings were pressing the young man's suit for him.

One afternoon the young people found themselves left quite alone together in a great drawing-room of the New Palace. It was Ferdinand's hour by careful arrangement, as he knew. And that made him perhaps even more shy than usual. But at length he managed the proposal. He lived, he said, in a far country. It was very lonely for him down there. And he wanted a wife. Would the Princess marry him? He moved nearer and put his arm about her.

So she was being offered, you see, a crown. In that was glamor enough for any girl of sixteen. It was also apparent how painfully difficult it had been for the royal suitor to get it said that he wanted her. A feeling akin to maternal compassion arose in her heart; a great wave of sympathy thrilled her. She sensed at once that here was a young man who needed assistance. She might supply that need. She visioned that far land of romance where they two should walk hand in hand and she would be an obedient wife and a genuine helpmate too.

Altogether flattered and pleased, it was not strange that the emotion which possessed the girl passed well enough for love. So she said, Yes. Then a little later the drawing-room door softly, slowly moved; and the Duchess, her hand on the knob, looked in. "Everything is all right," announced the relieved young suitor.

Like that, at Potsdam, May 22, 1892, she was engaged. At a great state dinner one night on the Island of Peacocks in one of the Potsdam lakes, the Kaiser himself announced the betrothal.

Well, and so they married her. First there was in June a visit to Schloss Sigmaringen, the ancient citadel on the Danube in Swabia in the highlands of Germany, which was the cradle of the Hohenzollern family and still the headquarters of the Roman Catholic branch. Here Missy was presented to Ferdinand's father, Prince Leopold, a charming middle-aged gentleman with a beard, and to his mother, a tall lady dressed in brown silk, the Princess Antoinette, who had been an Infanta of Portugal. There came also to look her over, of course, King Carol of Roumania, Leopold's brother, the uncle who had made Ferdinand his heir. Missy and Ducky, all dressed in their best, were taken to the station to meet the

King. They found him a bluff but amiable and hearty man, who wore very thick clothes and thick-soled boots. The gentlemen of his suite who accompanied him had all the grace of the Latin race, with the gift of paying pretty compliments to pretty girls. The King had brought for his future niece-in-law a splendid Roumanian embroidered costume, which he asked her to wear. Later it was to contribute not a little to making her the real Queen of Roumania that she has become.

Later at Sigmaringen there were long talks between the Duchess of Edinburgh and King Carol, at which were settled all the arrangements for the marriage. The Duke, who would have preferred the English marriage with George, his nephew, was not present. At last everything was settled satisfactorily and the Duchess was enchanted. At the feast that confirmed the coming alliance, King Carol lifted his glass and proposed the toast to the health and honeymoon ("one long honey day" he called it) of the young people.

Afterward King Carol and Ferdinand made a journey north to pay their respects at the English court. It was Missy herself, leading Ferdinand by the hand right into the room where the bullfinch lived, who presented her bridegroom to Grandmamma the Queen. Victoria, in her bunchy black silk gown, smiled encouragingly on him and gave him her fat little hand to kiss. As always it trembled a little. Ferdinand kept close by Missy's side throughout the visit, refusing to be interested in the shipyards and the English institutions that the King, his uncle, wished him to see. It was hardest of all for Missy when they had to meet Cousin George. Her white lids drooped over the eyes that in the garden of San Antonio had shone in such divine blue wonder.

The marriage Queen Victoria wished to have take place at Windsor or at St. George's in London. Then she herself would have given her granddaughter away. But that might not be, because Ferdinand was a Roman Catholic. It occurred January 10, 1893, at Sigmaringen.

It was a very splendid occasion for which guests assembled from all over Europe: royal highnesses, princes and princesses, ambassadors and generals and excellencies, dukes and archdukes and grand dukes, and all the highest connections from every royal house. The Queen of Roumania, Carmen Sylva, was ill at her own ancestral home at Neuwied. She sent a telegram of beautiful wishes for the happiness of the bride and groom, expressing her deep regret that she was not able to take part in the family festival. For foreign sovereigns it was not customary to leave their thrones. Queen Victoria was specially represented by the Duke of Connaught and the Czar of Russia by the Grand Duke Alexis. All of the Hohenzollerns were there, those of the Roman Catholic branch and those of the Protestant branch, with Kaiser Wilhelm the latter's most distinguished representative and the supreme head for the entire family. There were large delegations from the Hohenzollern principalities and from Roumania. Altogether the ceremony was witnessed by no less than 2,000 people.

The gifts were numerous and magnificent. The bride herself was dowered from Russia's rich treasury. When Marie Alexandrovna had married, there had been required a whole ship to carry to England her linen alone; it had been from this great store that her daughter was now outfitted. Also there was handed down the priceless wedding veil already worn by many a grand duchess.

They dressed Missy in her wedding clothes. Her gown was of heavy white silk embroidered with pearls. About her white throat they hung the costliest necklace of pearls. Her flowing veil was fastened with a richly jewelled diadem. Lastly they added the orange blossoms for her adorning.

The union of two great houses was announced by the booming of guns. Then the bells began to ring. They wedded her by ring and book and seal of state. There were words enough by chaplain and priest. Three times they wedded her. First occurred the civil ceremony performed with the legal requirements of the registry office. An hour later in the historic court chapel of all the Hohenzollerns, she knelt beside Ferdinand on an embroidered red velvet cushion before a gleaming altar. And the Roman Catholic church pronounced her a wife. Next, the long wedding procession wound its slow majestic way to the great Hall of the Ancestors, where had been set for the occasion candles and embroideries and all the proper accoutrements for English marriage. There the Established Church of England said over her all of the formulas that custom required. The ceremony was performed by Mr. Lloyd, the naval chaplain from the Duke's flagship, who had been selected by Queen Victoria for this purpose. The Duke of Edinburgh gave his daughter away.

It was finished. She was now no more Marie, Princess of Edinburgh of Great Britain and Ireland. Now she was Marie, Crown Princess of Roumania. And she had said "Yes," she tells me to-day, as lightly as when one consents to a long drive. "Smilingly, simply, stupidly," she says, "I stepped into my new life."

They parted her wedding veil. And she looked out a bride, a little child bride of seventeen. The height and the depth of experience awaited her. But of that she knew nothing at all. She was a nice little English girl. And no one ever told nice little English girls anything. The old German sagas, Andersen's Fairy Tales and Miss Young's books were all that she had read. So carefully had she been guarded from all true knowledge of life. And now to-night she would have to face it quite unprepared.

Well, there was a great banquet. Many toasts were drunk to the happiness and long life of the young couple, while the band played "Deutschland über Alles" and the Roumanian "Traiasca

Regale." The guests remained feasting until midnight. But at nine o'clock the bridal pair took their departure for the Castle de la Krauchenwies in the forest, a small castle like a hunting lodge where they were to spend their honeymoon. It was a brilliant cold winter's night. But the fur robes were thick and warm and deep. There was a drive of about an hour. The sleigh sped over a heavy white crust of snow, while a moon hung silver-gold overhead and stars sparkled and spangled the dark heavens. The drive was lovely. Missy liked it.

And then——! Louisa, her maid, was preparing her for the night. There were two beds, an empty waiting one beside her own. She had at length been tucked in. Now Louisa curtesied gravely. And making the sign of the cross, "Your Royal Highness, I shall pray for you," she said. Three times she curtesied and made the sign of the cross and repeated, "Your Royal Highness, I shall pray for you." Now whatever did Louisa mean by that?

Morning came. And Missy knew. All the veil of romance had been rent by reality. "That was a fool's paradise in which girls were brought up in those days," says the Queen of Roumania.

The festivities at Sigmaringen continued for more than a week. They closed with a great ball for which Ferdinand and his Princess returned. Then there was a brief visit to Coburg to say farewell to her family. The time for parting came.

The Duchess, who believed that "one must keep one's spirits up," tried to be gay. The Duke, usually a taciturn man, put his head on his little daughter's shoulder and sobbed that he could not bear to let her go. She was his favorite child. But really it was Ducky it was hardest to leave. A sick feeling of sadness came over Missy when she kissed this darling sister good-by. Also there was a flutter of fear at her heart. Roumania had been to her a mysterious land of romance. But now it appeared as a distant unknown country to which she was going with an unknown man. So she faced the future.

Lady Augusta Monson, for years her mother's lady-in-waiting, accompanied the little bride. It was by the arrangement of Queen Victoria, who delegated her to bring back a complete report about how the child was settled in her new surroundings. King Carol had sent his royal private train for the journey of the bridal party. There was a stop in Vienna, where they were entertained at the Austrian court by the Emperor Franz Joseph. In her trousseau Missy had many beautiful dresses and magnificent jewelry, all, to be sure, selected by her mother. But now she might wear whatever she chose. And she was almost as pleased as in the days at Malta when the "dressing-up basket" lent itself to the exercise of free choice in her own adorning. There was one misadventure that troubled her. Somehow, stepping from the railway carriage at Vienna, she stained her pink dress with grease. It seemed to her that all eyes were fixed on that spot.

At length the journey was resumed. Budapest was reached. The plains of Hungary were traversed. Sinaia was passed. And all the while the little bride was deciding and deciding over again what she should wear for the most important moment of her arrival in Bucharest, to which they were now drawing near. She finally had her maid put on a dull green velvet gown embroidered in gold. She wore a velvet coat of changing rose and gold and violet color, trimmed and lined with a superb white fox fur; and on her head a small toque in gold tissue ornamented with emeralds and rubies. When the locomotive, all draped in Roumanian and English national colors, pulled into the Gare du Nord at Bucharest, the entire nation was discovered to be making a festival of this memorable day. The bridal party was received by throngs of cheering people. There was a guard of honor, battalions of soldiers and a band from twenty-one regiments played the national anthem. All of Bucharest society was there and all of the officers of the army in brilliant uniforms and covered with decorations. Prince Ferdinand himself, in military uniform, gave his hand to his Princess to alight from the train. And she fairly tumbled out to fall into the arms of "Uncle." King Carol gave her a hearty kiss and folded her in his arms, charmed with the prize he had won for his kingdom.

Then Missy lifted her head and raised her eyes to look out on the vast throngs for which she was the center of interest. They were swarthy, dark-eyed, Latin, almost oriental. She was tall, fair, blue-eyed, golden-haired, northern, and young and seventeen. A wave of admiration thrilled through the crowd: "The top of the basket!" they murmured. "The top of the basket!"

Now among all the throng who looked on her that day, there was one whose gaze remained transfixed. It was as if the arrow of his adoration had fixed his heart. He was a young lieutenant in the guard of honor. Never before had he seen anything like her fair beauty. He was as one who might for the first time have seen the shining of the sun. He thrilled at the marvel that he witnessed. From that hour began the devotion he rendered as to a goddess divine.

The Mayor of Bucharest advanced, surrounded by his adjutants all in black and gold uniform and wearing silver chains. These attendants carried on a silver platter a loaf of barley bread and salt which, according to an ancient ceremony of welcome, was offered to their Royal Highnesses to partake of. Then in a specially constructed pavilion hung with crimson velvet and wreathed and twined with roses, His Majesty the King presented the young couple to the ministers of state and to the Roumanian nobility.

Now the cortege started for the Metropole, the cathedral on the hill, where their arrival would be signalized with a religious ceremony. The royal carriage, which led the rest, was drawn by six black horses. King Carol had the Princess at his side and Ferdinand sat facing them. Two outriders in grand livery preceded the carriage and there was an escort of soldiers. Through one green arch of triumph after another the procession passed. All the public buildings and the private houses of the city were draped with bunting in the Roumanian national colors, red, yellow and blue. Flags floated everywhere. The bridge across the Dumbavitza was lined with little fir trees. A rain of flowers fell constantly from the balconies beneath which the carriages passed. The sidewalks were packed with people making obeisance, to which the occupants of the royal carriage responded with continual bowing and smiling. The courtyard of the historical cathedral, the Metropole, was ornamented with escutcheons of the various districts of the country. Evergreen wreaths wound the fluted pillars of the entrance porch, which was decorated also with the arms of Roumania. The Metropolitan himself in splendid glittering robes stepped forth to receive the royal arrivals. There was a church service at which was sung the Te Deum in the mystical Greek orthodox measures that make the most beautiful religious music in the world.

Missy stepped up on a high dais covered with a Turkish carpet. She stood there, fair and white like a lily. But she was all enfolded in the richly

Byzantine eastern color that streamed everywhere about her from candle-lit painted ikons and through stained-glass windows. She faced the high gold altar screen inset with paintings of the twelve apostles and the Holy Family. From all the walls and the high-domed ceiling looked down upon her golden-haloed saints. Oh, how many saints there are you may never know until you have come yourself within the holy place of their presence in the Metropole on the hill at Bucharest. Here with the apostles and the Holy Family and all the saints looking down as a cloud of witnesses, Marie, Crown Princess of Roumania, kissed the silver cross, the wondrously wrought silver cross the Metropolitan held before her—and took up her marriage that would lead to a throne.

The wedding party left the cathedral acclaimed by great throngs of people shouting "Traiasca, long life!" They entered the palace between two rows of little girls holding high branches of flowers. That night the whole city was brilliantly illuminated in their honor. Followed two weeks of festivities, luncheons, dinners, dancing, balls, receptions, a gala performance at the opera house. Everywhere the beauty and grace and charm of the new Crown Princess, far beyond what they had even imagined, was the universal theme. And her lovely pictured face was being sold all over Bucharest.

And behind the palace walls a homesick little girl who had become Roumania's national possession turned often for consolation to a casket of foolish little things she had brought from her own north land. It held a blue bead from Venice, a little ivory image of a Buddha she had found once on the gravel path when she walked with her nursery governess in the Green Park, photographs of her home in Coburg, photographs of the picnic parties at St. Paul's Bay in Malta, and a twisted braid of hair from the tail of her first horse, Ruby. Besides, there was the crystal clock "from George to darling Missy" for whom her heart ached most.

Now that casket of foolish little things the Queen of Roumania has kept until this day. And as I have told you, she has only to look in the crystal and there fall from her shoulders all the cares of a kingdom and all the years of her royalty.

CHAPTER V

Her Royal Highness

POOR little girl, if only I might have been there to help her," said the Queen musingly.

Through the clear night air from down the mountain side came the rhythmic chanting of the monks at prayer. We both listened softly. And the golden room was still. I looked across at the mobile, expressive face of the woman on the divan, whose courage of soul is perhaps her most outstanding characteristic. I wondered. Isn't she all that she is to-day, perhaps just because that little Crown Princess who went before had to stand on her own feet and grow strong in a struggle of the spirit that fitted her at last to face life unflinchingly?

Still, one must sympathize with seventeen. For seventeen could not know how everything that was happening was eventually going to be good for her like that. The two weeks of festivities that had greeted her arrival were over. All the dance music had suddenly stopped. A kingdom had returned to its daily affairs.

The Palatul Victorei, the main Roumanian royal residence, seemed to the girl who had come to live in it fairly to echo with its own silences. The palace stands in the heart of Bucharest facing the Calea Victorei. Previously occupied by princes who had gone before, it had been enlarged and remodelled to its present form by King Carol. Exteriorly it is a quite plain two story structure with a mansard roof, and covered like other Roumanian residences with a stucco that gleams white in the southern sun. It is built long and rectangularly about three sides of an open court, the center of which is ornamented with a fountain. And the whole is enclosed with a high iron fence, before the gates of which are always pacing the sentries in uniform, each carrying a gun over his shoulder.

Inside you find the palace much more regal. The rooms are high and handsome. Anyone who tries to tell you how many loses count. But they are something like seventy in number. These include some that are great halls like the *Salle de Musique* with its built-in organ at which Carmen Sylva used to play; the library, its walls lined with books gleaming red and gold in beautiful bindings; the banquet hall hung with Gobelin tapestries and affording seating capacity for 500 people; the ball room glittering with crystal chandeliers; and immediately adjoining and of course most impressive of all, the throne room, where beneath a crimson canopy on the high gold chairs, Their Majesties sit when receiving in state. Throughout the palace there is much heavily-panelled and carved dark woodwork. There are many bronzes. And everywhere the walls are hung with old religious paintings, so many of which portray suffering and tragedy.

To the girl who came up the great marble staircase here a bride, this that was to be her home seemed all solemnly austere, all overwhelmingly oppressive. And the apartments set apart for their young Royal Highnesses were not different from the rest. A massive, wide, German four-poster occupied their bedroom. In the sitting room were chairs and sofas so heavy they seemed not made to be rested upon. Looking back on it all to-day, the Queen says: "There was nowhere I could make a cozy corner of any kind. The false elegance drove me mad. I would have loved a peasant's room with white-washed walls. I wanted a bare space where I could have set a bowl of roses on a table."

Ultimately Missy would be making her own place in this Roumania. At this time, however, she must accept that which had been prepared for her. Back there in the hotel parlor at Munich, when the Crown Prince had first spoken of his far country, it had held for her all of the fascination of distant places. But now that she was here, as she looked around, all that charm seemed to have vanished like a mirage. Sometimes she stood at a palace window and watched the passers-by. She might have been, it seemed to her, a monument in a public square, a statue in stone. Just about as near as that she felt to any living contact with this alien environment. She was highly prized and valued and admired, to be sure. There was no doubt about that, with a nation acclaiming her beauty.

But a nation was not what she needed. Can you sob out your loneliness to the heart of a nation or sing out your joy to it? Out there, always going by, were people who knew each other; people who looked into people's eyes; people who touched people's hands; people who laughed with people and could weep with people; all of these people always going by, were people who had people that cared.

And she was apart in her high place, a Crown Princess, to be approached with form and ceremony. More, she must herself observe all forms and ceremonies that set this distance between her and the rest of the world about her. Could the royal household within its carefully guarded enclosures afford sufficient compensation by way of companionship? Ferdinand, the young husband, it is true, did not fail to place convincing kisses on the ripe red lips. King Carol meant to be kind. But Ducky, her beloved sister, was not there. And a single day without Ducky in it still held an aching void she had not yet learned to fill. She wanted the sound of Ducky's voice calling, "Missy, Oh, Missy!" She wanted the feel of Ducky's fingers in hers, as hand in hand they would go tripping happily along a garden path.

So long as Lady Monson remained, she was not

yet quite cast adrift and alone in her new existence. Lady Monson, in pursuance of that mission on which she had been sent, was acquainting herself with this Roumania of which she was to carry back the report to Queen Victoria. Palace doors did not shut her in. They swung easily for her to pass. Many functions were given for her. And she would come back from all sorts of delightful social occasions bringing anecdotes and pleasant things to hear, for which the little Royal Highness in her gilded cage wistfully waited. She herself, you see, might not go out like this to play about at will and drink tea with whomsoever she might please. Nobody could ever ask her. Nobody of course dared to. Inexorable were the regal restrictions. Tradition as sacred as unwritten forbade that royalty should appear at any social function in a mere private residence, even in a residence of Bucharest's elect nobility or at a legation. And it was going to be yet some time before Marie of Roumania would be strong enough in her soul to break all the red tape that wound her away from human kind. It was for nearly fifteen years, she tells me, that she kept the royal social code.

For the present, in this day of her youth, she found herself a stranger in a strange land, glimpses of which she was glad to get through another's eyes. But from even this diversion she would soon be cut off. Lady Monson would be going at the end of six weeks, leaving her more lonely and homesick than ever.

But that, after all, was a plain and simple sort of suffering. It was not to be compared with a really terrifying prospect that the future already held. There was sickness that was not nostalgia. Every morning now the little Princess found herself ill, oh, so dreadfully ill. "It seems so strange," she said to Lady Monson. "It is in the morning. And then in the afternoon I am all right. But every morning again, I am ill."

Lady Monson listened and looked at the girl. Was she then such a child that she didn't know? She hadn't the least idea? It was on the day that Lady Monson was leaving for England: "Missy," she said, "don't you know what is the matter?"

But Missy certainly didn't. Then Lady Monson told her. And the blue eyes opened wide in surprise and fear. Must this then so soon befall her? She had been married six weeks. Now it was coming, that unknown mysterious event, for which she was so totally unprepared that she had never before even heard of the portents that announce its advent. Even so, the months were already steadily measuring off her time. The hour of woman's supreme experience was bearing down upon her. She had relatives, mind you, who sat upon all the thrones of Europe. Yet she felt just as alone and friendless as might a bride in a Bronx flat.

Now Lady Monson had gone. From the Roumanian court had been appointed a lady-in-waiting to the Crown Princess. But the lady was, after all, a foreigner. There was really only the English maid Louisa whom she had brought with her, with whom Missy could talk. And Louisa was an old maid! No other woman was near for advice or counsel. The Roumanian Queen Elizabeth, "Carmen Sylva," was still ill in Germany. Most of that first year the girl lived through with just two men. Into her eyes now had come a look of settled hopeless despair. During the days she cried a great deal. For the long evenings, she sat and listened while her husband and "Uncle" talked politics and military affairs and smoked long black cigars she could not endure.

King Carol worked early and long in his office, an imposing room with dark, heavily-carved woodwork and with stained-glass windows glowing with pictures of martyrs and saints and crusaders. The desk at which he sat was of carved walnut, the heavy flat top resting on two massive, carved, crouching lions. It was so large that it had been necessary to have it built in the room. The King had with his own hands assisted in its construction. He was proud of his skill as an excellent carpenter and joiner.

Well, here at this desk, he used to sit day by day building a kingdom. And his nephew and heir he desired to have stand by. The King was wholly, completely absorbed in his task. He lived a life that was austere, simple, selfless—and expected other people to also. The Crown Prince

he had trained with German thoroughness to follow methodically in his footsteps. Explicit obedience to his instructions had been so inculcated
that Uncle's will had become law for Ferdinand.
In an office adjoining that of the King he too
busied himself faithfully in the execution of tasks
laid out for him. All of this routine, which was of
Uncle Carol's ordering, was as regular as clock-
work.

In this rigid atmosphere, the lonely girl found
her days long, long days. Just one deviation the
daily schedule afforded by way of her entertainment. It was the afternoon drive out the Calea
Victorei and along the Chaussee Kisselef, the
boulevard that was Bucharest's fashionable prome-
nade. But Ferdinand started always about an
hour ahead of time, thus missing all the bright
throng with their Paris gowns and their gaiety.
"But why, Nanda, do we go so early?" asked the
girl. Well, he didn't like to be stared at. And
wasn't it an awful bore to be kept constantly smiling and bowing and returning salutations? No,
for the Crown Princess it was not. For her the
people would never be too many. And never
would she find their attentions irksome. But the
time of the ride could not be different. At the
same hour at which they had started the first day,
they went regularly every day. It was not ever
easy for Nanda to change. He was like that.

Once, beside the daily ride, there was a visit to
a monastery. They went in a coach drawn by the

four cream-colored horses with black tails. The monastery wasn't very exciting. But still, here was something being done. Aside from this event, nothing else happened. Nothing at all ever happened. It was the lady-in-waiting who finally went to the King and suggested that for a young thing like the Crown Princess there ought to be some sort of social life. So much loneliness and grief were not good for the state of her health. So it was arranged that Her Royal Highness should give at the Palace a series of teas.

How Missy wished now she had paid more attention to that French language she and Ducky had so giggled about as the affectation of grown-ups. She had to use it now, since she did not yet know Roumanian. All of the upper classes here spoke French. From France also they had adopted their manners and customs. At her first ball Missy had observed with questioning surprise the rouged cheeks and carmined lips of the ladies. This was, of course, in the days before all of the Anglo-Saxon world had done it. Up in the land that Victoria ruled a painted woman could not be received in polite society. Once Missy remembered to have heard Grandmamma the Queen pronounce a woman like that a "Jezebel." And now here at the court that would some day be hers, at these very functions at which she was now presiding, women were coming that way, ladies of the highest nobility. There would be more that it would be hard for her English conventionality to adjust itself to in the Latin race, the broad jest which so invariably adorns their repartee, the utter absence of reticence about matters which Anglo-Saxons with dropped eyes prefer to pass over in silence.

Missy had dressed for the last of her teas in a violet velvet gown, with its so fashionable bell skirt and enormous balloon sleeves. And she put on the turquoises her father had given her. She looked very lovely. But the dress, she noticed, was growing tight. What occurred, therefore, was not from the eastern point of view surprising. It was even to have been expected. Right in the midst of the tea when conversation had waxed most elegant, it happened. A fat dowager, beaming with a suggestive smile, planted herself fairly in front of the Crown Princess, to announce clearly in a voice that all might hear: "Your Royal Highness, since your condition is no longer a mystery, may we felicitate you upon it?" And overwhelmed with embarrassment, the English girl replied by bursting into tears.

Next, Easter was coming. On Good Friday, since their confirmation, she and Ducky had always gone together to Holy Communion. Now in Bucharest she would be going alone. Her pew at the Lutheran church was all decorated with hyacinths and lilies. When the congregation stood up to say the Lord's Prayer, she stood too. And suddenly she had dropped in a heap on the floor. They carried her to the church porch and with the touch of the cool spring air on her face,

she came out of the faint. They took her home.
And Bucharest, and all Roumania with it, began
to rejoice. From now on, all the country would
be waiting to see whether the English Princess
would provide an heir to the throne.

Up at Sinaia stood the castle in the forest that
was the royal summer residence. All around it
the wild flowers were springing up in the grass.
All around it the wild birds were calling from
the trees. On a certain day in June each year
the royal household with unvarying German regu-
larity moved to Sinaia. "Oh, no," Nanda had insisted with alarm, "it wouldn't be possible to go
any earlier. It wouldn't be of the least use to ask
Uncle. No one could go to Sinaia until the day
came. No one ever did." This was a household
of habit, and everyone who lived in it was expected to have the habit. So Missy, who so loved
the out-of-doors and every wild thing in it, must
be content to wait and watch the calendar.

Great Castle Pelash she found in June another
stately residence in the German style that King
Carol loved. The feature of the music room is the
beautiful piano in the form of a golden harp, in-
vented and designed by Carmen Sylva herself.
Castle Pelash, you realize, is probably as these
two wished it. Even more heavily carved and pan-
elled it is than the Palatul Victorei, with woodwork of that wonderful coloring and satin soft
texture that is due wholly to the loving touch and
the native skill of German craftsmanship. It

makes rooms with deep shadows, rooms that are mysteriously enchanting when illumined with a slanting shaft of sunlight. But on dark days they seem to stand emptily silent and sullen and severe. They are, however, always excellently adapted to one purpose: down these countless long corridors, up the great staircases and in and out of the dark recesses, Missy's children have through the years all of them played hide and seek. She herself, the first spring that she came here, I think found the great Castle Pelash a little forbidding. She preferred the green mountain side and all the blue arched sunlit out-of-doors. She and Nanda together sought violets and anemones on the wide green lawns. In the evenings Uncle Carol and Nanda played billiards while she sat by and listened to the click-click of the balls.

At last Ducky, the dearest thing on earth, was coming for a visit. But Missy looked down with dismay at her figure. What should she say about it? She decided to say nothing. Nanda got out the four cream-colored horses, and they drove all the way to the frontier to meet Ducky. The two girls hugged each other and cried for joy. The past winter the Duchess of Edinburgh, in an effort to make Ducky forget her grief at the parting with her beloved sister, had taken this daughter for a gay season to the court at St. Petersburg. And the girl had been told to write to Roumania only casual, pleasant letters with all the tears left out.

But all the time, she now declared, her heart had been breaking for Missy.

The day for which a nation breathlessly waited was approaching. The Duchess of Edinburgh had come for the occasion. Queen Victoria had sent her own personal court physician, a Dr. Fairplay. Previously there had been much correspondence between her and King Carol. Now she sent a telegram demanding that he accept for her granddaughter the English doctor's service. Sternly disapproving, the King was at the last moment compelled to capitulate.

The point of their discussion and their differences concerned the use of chloroform in childbirth. This was still so new that Queen Victoria at the birth of her own ninth child had been the first woman in the world to benefit by it. Only because she was a sovereign had she been able to command and secure it, and so set the precedent that was to mitigate for succeeding generations of women something of the ages' long curse. In her own day, Her Majesty's achievement had been in defiance of both science and religion. The medical profession itself had demurred. The clergy had hurled their anathema against the use of the anesthetic: was it not divinely decreed that woman should pay, pay, pay for the apple that Eve did eat? Any alleviation of that agony was flying in the face of providence and was contrary to all religion. In 1893 church and state down in Roumania still felt that way. Roumanian physicians declined to lend their assistance to any such subversive doctrine. Dr. Fairplay took command of the case.

To the great state bedroom at Castle Pelash which had been set apart for the entertainment of visiting Kings and Emperors, they brought Missy at night. In the morning of October 15, at just about dawn, she had finished her task. The Prime Minister, expecting to witness and attest the event, arrived too late. At six o'clock the cannon at the capitol were firing their salute. Anxiously the listening city counted. By tradition and custom, 21 guns would announce the arrival of a mere girl. But that feeble mark was passed. The cannon boomed on. Hurrah! It would be a boy!

The cheering rose in a mighty chorus. And before the requisite 101 guns proclaiming the great advent could be completed, the populace in a frenzy of excitement was dancing the Hora in the streets of Bucharest. The glad news of an heir was relayed throughout the land. From the farthest mountains and plains the bells rang out to a kingdom the message of jubilee. At Sinaia the triumphant pealing of the monastery chimes was the first sound that broke upon the consciousness of the girl in the great carved bed. Drifting back from the black bottomless pit of maternity, she opened questioning blue eyes: "Unto you a son is born," they said.

And she turned her face to the wall. The bells! The bells! The bells! They went ringing on.

So this was what they'd wanted her for, she said in her bitter young heart. Now they'd got what they were after.

She felt as if she'd been trapped in the dark. Her youth had been so torn asunder with pain. She was voicing her first burning resentment. But when she felt the soft little bundle they laid at her side she was ready to take up her woman's burden. Suddenly she loved her baby passionately. She snatched him to her heart. And she thought long, long thoughts. Some day he would sit upon the throne. Bone of her bone, flesh of her flesh, she had created a king!

They christened him at the castle with all the ceremony of the Greek Orthodox Church. They named him Carol after the founder of the dynasty. The Crown Prince was a Roman Catholic. The Crown Princess still retained her membership in the English Established Church. But their children, it had been agreed, were to be Roumanians of the Roumanians. They have therefore all been brought up in the Greek Orthodox faith. The baptism is always by immersion. So now in a deep basin of water set on a table, the naked baby was dipped three times, the officiating priest deftly with three fingers covering eyes and mouth. The child was then anointed with oil.

The high nobility and the dignitaries of the kingdom were there. But the mother was not present. Not yet had been completed the days of her "purification." She must be "churched," you know. The ceremony in the Greek church is very similar to that in the English church. The Crown Princess, when her time came, went like any lesser woman.

Carol had been christened on her eighteenth birthday. In less than a year, Elizabeta had been born. And then there was an interval for her own growing up.

Carmen Sylva had returned to take her place in the royal household. But her advent contributed little to Missy's happiness. There was between these two what in effect amounted to the relationship of mother-in-law and daughter-in-law with its historic difficulties. One was the setting and the other the rising star. Besides, the older woman had for twenty-seven years failed to give the country an heir. And the girl had in nine months achieved it.

It has been said that no house is ever large enough for two families. Well, even a palace isn't. It was evident that the young people of the royal household required their own domestic ménage. Up at Sinaia, Castle Pelasor was ultimately built for their summer residence. And in Bucharest, the Cotroceni palace was set in order for their occupancy. Other remodelling has since been done from time to time, so that to-day this beautiful palace reflects much of Queen Marie's artistic instinct and skill. On the outskirts of the city, it had formerly served as a summer residence for Prince Cuza, the ruler who preceded King Carol. He it was who had abolished the religious orders in Roumania, and so he had not hesitated to convert to his own purpose what had been originally an old monastery.

The palace to-day, three stories high and as usual rectangular, is built upon the foundations of the monks' cells, which formerly were ranged about the three sides of the courtyard, in which still stands the basilica. This is a lovely ancient little sanctuary rich with embroideries and ikons and Byzantine paintings of the saints. Before its altar, the swinging lamps of silver and gold are still burning as for the 300 years since its founding. The name Cotroceni means "heavy roots," and conveys the idea of the work involved in clearing the ground for the first building. It is trees from the primeval forest that make the wooded park here where the nightingales sing. And the grounds have been landscaped and adorned with terraced gardens that slope away and away to frame in the distance a vista of Bucharest.

Within, the palace is a skillful combination of simplicity and splendor. From rooms with quiet plastered walls in the old Roumanian style, you may pass to the dining room with walls and furniture all done in antique gold, or to the beautiful gold salon with turquoise blue walls and ceiling all overlaid with branching trees sculptured in gold. But for the gem of the entire palace, you should see the Queen's own private apartment.

At Versailles or at Schönbrunn, Marie Antoinette or Maria Theresa achieved nothing so distinctive as this which has been done at Cotroceni for the enshrinement of a beautiful woman. A studio with a carved, beamed ceiling and with hangings and upholstery in rich eastern combinations of plum color and purple and gold and green, is reminiscent of ancient mosques and old temples. In the bedroom adjoining, you have arrived at the real sanctuary of life. The effect of the room is to make one feel that it was made for moonlight and all soft silvery silences. The woodwork, in ivory tone and exquisitely carved, is an exhibit in craftsmanship that bears testimony to the versatility of the Queen: she with her sister Ducky, the Grand Duchess Cyril of Russia, spent hours and days in its personal execution. The cathedral ceiling, arched and vaulted, is sculptured with branching trees, the whole overlaid in silver. Here and there swing dim, burning, antique lamps of wrought silver. On the floor of blue tile are set in a few wide spaces silver braziers brimming with flowers. The bed, with a headboard in the shape of a silvered Greek cross, is a low couch which stands on a dais beneath a high, carved, ivory canopy. It is covered with streaming precious stuffs, fabrics of marvellously woven threads of purple and gold and silver. The bed faces at the opposite side of the room a fireplace and mantel, above which is a painting, also the work of the Grand Duchess Cyril. The picture of scattered anemone blooms is cleverly illumined by a row of concealed tiny electric bulbs, so that it is the first sight on which the Queen from her couch opens her eyes in the morning. And beneath the anemones she reads the lettered inscription: "Once it was always springtime in my heart."

This is the palace which the Queen and the present royal family have lived in most. Over the main staircase is the portrait that shows Marie a bride at seventeen. In the gold salon, she appears in her Roumanian costume. Here you see her with her first child in her arms. There she is with the mystery of a fuller maturity in her eyes. It is as if at every turning, as you move through this palace, you are meeting the pictured presence of which the beautiful woman you know to-day is the reality. Only she is no longer any one of them. She is all of them. And here it was she found her soul.

She had come here to Roumania to a land she did not know and a husband she did not know. For the first two years she had tacitly accepted her environment in a stern stiff court. But with her return to normal health, her old joy in life began to assert itself once more. Yet how should she express it? In this atmosphere of awful, regular routine, it was King Carol's iron will that directed every activity. He believed in work and in keeping women in their place. The very idea of amusement seemed sacrilegious. Nearly everything desirable appeared to be "verboten." And she was a young thing, eager and gay, who began to strain at the captivity of rules and regulations around her. The man she had married, on the contrary, had been brought up under them, trained to them. He had followed them always with implicit obedience. Ferdinand was a conformist. And she! The very essence of the charm of her has always been a quality of spirit a little primitive, untamed, unconventional. She as a little girl could no more have been stopped from climbing trees in the Gardens of San Antonio than you could have stopped the squirrels. It has never been possible to manipulate her to any prevailing mode; when the dressmakers of Paris have tried it she has flouted their fashions. She can never be reduced to a pattern, even a royal pattern, as her ministers of state have learned.

In those early days at Cotroceni, two young people pronounced one for reasons of state and decreed until death to walk side by side through life, discovered themselves to be as diverse in temperament as if the wide world had held them apart. She was active, impulsive, magnetic, dynamic, daring. He was shy, reticent, methodical, deliberate, conservative; he was content with the beaten path. And she! Oh, she was most of all a pathfinder, before whose eager feet new ways would ever unfold.

Two interests they had in common: photography in a day when the kodak was yet new and nearly all young people were snapshotting; and flowers, which it wouldn't have been German for Ferdinand not to have cared for and for which Marie had a passion. As recently as a year ago said the King to the Queen: "What shall I give you, my dear, for your birthday?" And she did not ask for jewels. "I want irises," she said. And he got her fifteen thousand bulbs from Holland.

In their younger days, they always went out together to find the first flowers of spring. Now it might be the beauty of a blossom by the roadside or the beauty of a sunset in the sky; wherever she saw beauty, it moved Missy. So that she felt as if she must have some other soul to scream it out to, to make it more beautiful. She tried sometimes like this to scream it to Nanda. Now Nanda liked flowers, it is true, but he seldom talked about them. And well, he didn't exactly understand what all the noise was about.

What worried him more was the unusual things that Missy was always wanting to do. Why not ride out and see the peasants? It would be nice to know how they kept their houses and how they made their clothes. Nanda in haste protested: "Perhaps Uncle might not like it."

"But I'm not afraid of Uncle," she insisted. That was always her answer. And always he was chiding her for the very irregular things she was so constantly thinking up to do.

At last one day she said with a laugh: "Nanda, I shall tell you a story. There was once," she went on, "a German Prince who came courting a Russian Grand Duchess. He was all jammed up inside. And she was just all brimming over.

Well, he married her like that. And then he
wanted to change her. 'But,' she objected, 'if you
should change me, I wouldn't any more be what I
am. And it's what I am you fell in love with.'

"That's the way we are, Nanda," she concluded.
"You're all jammed up. I'm all brimming over.
And I'll just have to go on being what I am."

But she let him too go on being what he was.
And she didn't try to make him over. She had
insight, this girl. And vision wide enough to see
another's point of view. Even when she couldn't
accept it. So perhaps was steadied a marriage
that might otherwise have stranded.

Missy herself went on her own way, brimming
with light and life and laughter, and believing in
joy and her right to happiness. And she wasn't
afraid of Uncle, ever.

That had first been manifest the previous summer at Sinaia. The old King used to sit long at
luncheon expounding political matters. Everybody had to listen. And on and on he talked in-
terminably, really entertaining no one but himself. The Crown Princess conformed as long as
she could. Then one day she rose in her place,
remarking: "Uncle, you'll be good enough to ex-
cuse me. I have a lot to do. So I'll wish you good
afternoon."

Carmen Sylva looked plainly her disapproval.
Nanda sat rigid, at shocked attention for what
would happen. And then: "Oh, very well, Missy.
Good afternoon."

But it was the first time that anyone had ever questioned a program of the King's imposing. Some one who could rather interested him. He half turned his head for another glance at the disappearing figure of the girl with the vivid personality that was to lend color to his court.

That winter there began to be a good deal of entertaining at Cotroceni. Dances and cotillions and costume balls followed in gay succession. There was a fixed income for the household of the Crown Prince, and the King had assigned a financial secretary for the administration of it. But by spring many unpaid bills were piling up. The secretary came to His Royal Highness in real concern. What was to be done about it? The Crown Princess, observing her husband's worried expression, asked: "What's the matter, Nanda?"

"Why, you see," he replied, knitting his brows over the report that lay before him, "our revenue is too small." That seemed a little vague. She turned to the secretary, who explained: "Your Royal Highness, the trouble is the unpaid bills."

"Well," she demanded, "why aren't they paid at once?"

"Your Royal Highness," answered the secretary, "because there remains nothing with which to pay. You can see," he pointed out, "here are kitchen bills, the children's bills, florists' bills, all kinds of household bills, and your own personal bills. And it's because your personal expenditures are so very high that I cannot pay the others."

The Crown Princess's mother had been a rich woman, so very rich that never before had the girl felt any limit to money. But now she looked thoughtful. She knew how much she liked beautiful clothes, and good horses with fine harnesses, and expensive bulbs from Holland for her garden. And these things must, to be sure, cost money.

But she looked again at the secretary's report. "Why," she said, "but see here! My bills aren't paid either. So how can it be that the reason the kitchen bills aren't paid is because my bills take all the money?"

Oh, it was all a hopeless tangle to the feminine mind. But one thing the Crown Princess could see clearly: these were what were called debts. The royal household of Cotroceni was in debt, and was going to be more so. "Nanda," she said desperately, "you'll have to do something."

When Ferdinand didn't know what, she added firmly: "Then you'll have to tell Uncle." Afterward, two or three times she asked if he had told Uncle. Not yet, but he would. Three or four times, she asked. But it hadn't been done. Five or six times. At last it seemed ten times.

Then one day, when Ferdinand had gone a-hunting, she summoned the secretary. She was twenty. And she stood on her own feet. She has never forgotten that day. It was the first assertion of that personality which was later to sway a kingdom. "These bills," she said. "You and I will do what's got to be done. Maybe I do spend a lot of

128

money. Why did you let me? Anyhow, we'll face the music together and right now. I'm going to open the ball. But you've got to follow. Come along!"

They entered the room where the King sat at the massive desk with the crouching lions. Missy lifted her head high and looked squarely into the hard, stern eyes. "Your Majesty," she began, "some one has to tell you. Ferdinand won't. So I will. For some reason or other we're awfully in debt. And probably I'm the reason. If there's a spendthrift in the family, it must be me. For Nanda doesn't really need much or want much. But me, I want a lot. Only, more than that, I want to be honest. I can't bear to owe money. See," she said, as the secretary advanced and laid the bills on the table. "Now, what can we do about it? It's awful, the money we owe!"

But when she recounted the event afterward to Ferdinand, he had protested: "But why did you tell him you were extravagant?" "Because," she insisted, "it's best always to tell the whole truth, right out. I didn't want to have to be going back one day after another to add, 'Oh, to-day there's another three hundred pound bill that I forgot.' I wanted him to know just how it was, so there wouldn't be anything left to be told. So I said right out, it was awful, the money we owed."

The King had been very much surprised. And more, really, at the girl than at the situation she

129

had presented. But he didn't rage at all. He was quite calm, as were the lions beneath the table. "Well, I'll tell you what you will have to do," he said. "I'm going to loan you the money to pay off these debts. And there mustn't be any more. You'll now have to live on your revenue and somehow save out of it besides sufficient to pay me back."

Well, they did. I think that the King even charged them interest. But so, the Crown Princess learned economy. And from the moment that she had faced him fearlessly across his desk with her confession that day, an understanding had been established between her and Uncle.

Later, word came to Missy that the King to one of his ministers had said: "There's good stuff in that girl!"

CHAPTER VI

A Girl on Horseback

IT was with a laughing cry she had challenged
them: "Follow me who will! Catch me who
can!"

She was off with the wind. On her fleet-footed
horse she had whirled away ahead of them, all the
officers of the Czar's crack regiment. And they
were in hot pursuit. They skimmed over the hills
and slid through the valleys in thick clouds of dust
raised by their speeding horses' hoofs. But the
girl rode always in the lead. Racing madly as they
could, the foremost man had missed her by more
than twice his arm's length. She had finished the
course and whirled with her foam-flecked steed.
From a green hillock she faced them all.

Brilliant Russian sunshine burnished her hair
to its brightest gold. Her eyes flashed wide in
their deepest blue. Her cheeks glowed crimson
with high color. A vivid, panting, breathless
figure, the landscape held her against its background transfigured with her youth. She was a
creature all glorious. It was there for her to
read in the concentrated glance of all those oncoming men. And their flaming desire of her set

her pulses throbbing to a strange new tempo. The coronation of an Emperor had become the occasion really of Missy's debut, the coming out of the Crown Princess of Roumania for all Europe to see. And it had been as sudden as when a butterfly that has been a chrysalis finds wings.

At Moscow for the crowning of the last Czar that ever would be, all royalty and nobility were assembled. The festivities were lasting for three weeks. Guests were being entertained on the vast country estates of the Grand Dukes. All kinds of amusements were organized. But most of all, everybody rode. From the time of her little girlhood, with her Arabian pony, Ruby, down in Malta, Missy had loved a good horse and known how to handle one. Now in the joy of her release from the restrictions that prevailed at Bucharest, her bright nature bubbled over and burst all bounds. A zest for pleasure tautened and tuned every fiber of her being. Her fearlessness as a horsewoman had been already established as she rode successfully, splendidly, one after another of the most difficult chargers the Russian royal stables afforded.

It was useless for Ferdinand to counsel caution. She had thrown caution to the winds. She preferred to take courage instead, as she would from now on for all the days of her life.

Every man was wishing to loan her his mount. And when an officer with the fiercest, most fiery, Cossack horse of all came forward with his, she said, "Yes, thank you," and took that too. Then it was she had challenged them all to the chase that none had been able to win. Elusive, beyond their reach, she held them there at bay. And the distance that she set only served to enhance all the compelling lure of her. So her fascination grew.

To the daring recklessness of her horsemanship was added the divine rhythm of her dancing. And there was the destiny, you know, of her inheritance, brains and beauty and charm, that was drawing all men unto her. Her surpassing beauty became the cynosure for all attention at this most sumptuous court. All the loveliness that reigned in the kingdoms of a continent was here, set forth with every device for women's adorning, richly jewelled, glitteringly diademed. And clearly one woman led all the rest. Proof of it? The tribute in every man's eyes—and the protest in every woman's.

For the ceremonial installation of a ruler they had come. But something perhaps of even more import than the inauguration of Nicholas II was also occurring. In the echo of that gaiety with which ancient palaces rang, the princess who should rule through the hearts of men was to find her high place. Thereafter, no royal occasion would be complete without her coming. At the crowning of King Edward in England they greeted her: "Now we are happy in that you who are so joyous are here." The ripple of her laughter and the radiance of her presence gave her precedence at every court. Two kinds of women there are in the world: those who are loved, and those who art not. Probably not since Helen of Troy or Cleopatra has there been a more desired woman than Marie of Roumania. What had thrilled her pulses when she faced the oncoming riders who were her pursuers in that reckless race on horseback, what she had seen in their eyes, was the story that men were to tell her for the rest of her life. The charm of her! The charm of her! It was to bring a continent to her feet. Even from another continent, there have been those who also ran. The chase of her! The chase of her, the most elusive, most beautiful woman of her time! It has given her a supremacy that is not mere vanity of vanities; it is a chiefest feminine source of strength for the best achievement in life.

From the Kremlin crowning in Moscow, Missy returned to Bucharest, awake to the full awareness of herself as a woman. It had been a coming out indeed that was to make her the toast of Europe. Not the sparkle of the champagne, nor the fealty so easily sworn by those who have touched tinkling glasses, however, holds the high light for history. It is the woman who walks in beauty. That way lies power. The index of a feminine sense of it invariably appears in a certain sureness and firmness of tread. See the Queen of Roumania to-day. It is not by chance she is possessed of that depth of consciousness which has so given poise to her step and her soul.

Love is a votive offering which, laid at the shrine of the heart, makes all personality unfold. One man there was, who to this lady said very persistently that prayer. For the space of four years, every day and every year there arrived in the royal mail a letter fragrant with the incense of his devotion. Now his were on gold crested stationery of heavy cream texture. Others without benefit of emblem of lineage had been indited by a railway porter: this humble admirer, only having seen her pass by, took pen in hand and searching his memory for a simile with which to set forth her deliciousness, he wrote that she was "like unto a damson plum." No class or station, you see, is exempt. Even just so she affects them all. You remember how we told off our daisy petals: "doctor, lawyer, merchant, chief." The Queen needs a new one: kings and generals and poets and porters and peers, hers should begin. And hard as they would be to rhyme in, there'd have to be somewhere a place for a gentleman from Virginia and more who may not be forgot.

This is a woman possessed of an endowment conferring the experience that enriches life and develops capacities. But by inevitable corollary, there are responsibilities, difficulties too. "I rejoice in my beauty," the Queen said to me as we talked. "Men have taught me to."

Then she added in a voice that trailed off retrospectively almost as if she were seeing her own self go by down the past of her girlhood and womanhood: "But, you see, I have had to hold my head high. I've had to learn to go through life at times with level eyes lest I light in other eyes the fire that might not be put out."

Ah, she has been able to ask much of life and richly receive it, this woman adored of her generation. Yet with men always at her feet, she has had to watch her step, lest at any time she trip. But knowledge like that comes with years. "At first, when one is very young and doesn't know, how can it really be helped?" says the Queen. "But when one grows older and knows what is going to happen, one walks of course, more carefully. After the romance is over, there will be always reality to be reckoned with. Is the dream worth the price you'll pay? For one way or another, you will always pay. Like that you can reason, when you have learned. Then it's up to you to decide whether you will or you won't—and abide by the consequences. But after you know, never again after you know, do you trip blindly into trouble."

Well, it was there at the Kremlin that Missy had in the exuberance of her youth for the first time "taken her head." She knew now her right to happiness. She could never again be coerced into cramping her joyous nature in a colorless existence.

Old King Carol had made her the Honorary Colonel of a regiment. Here she was in her element. From the time the Buckingham Palace

nurses, in stiff white piqué, had taken her to watch
the changing of the palace guard, she had adored
a soldier. How she thrilled now as in her smart
military uniform she sat on her horse at the moment of parade to watch these her own men pass
by in review. And for the first time since her
coming to Roumania there awoke in her heart a
sense of personal pride and possession. To these
at last she "belonged," and they to her. There was
no doubt but that the feeling was quite reciprocal.
For their beautiful Crown Princess an army would
have gone gladly to victory or to death. The girl
would have loved herself to have led them to
battle. The Queen's eyes flashed as she tells me
about it to-day. Since that might not be, Missy
had found an outlet for her spirits in riding often
with the officers of her regiment. Sometimes she
galloped away and away ahead of them with that
daring challenge she had flung to the breeze in
Russia: "Follow me who will."

There was one in particular who did. He had
been in that guard of honor, the young lieutenant
who had stood at transfixed attention, spellbound,
that day the glory of her fair beauty first burst
upon him as she stepped from the train on her
arrival in Bucharest, a bride. Other events had
since brought them into a companionship that
grew closer. It was not his doing, nor hers. Nor
was anyone at all at fault. Not long after their
Royal Highnesses had been settled in the new
home at Cotroceni, Ferdinand had developed a

severe illness. The doctors said it was going to be a long run of typhoid. It seemed desirable that there be some one officially appointed for special service for the household, some one to whom the Crown Princess might turn for any emergency assistance. And the young lieutenant had been chosen by King Carol himself.

It was that way he came. Not an appointment to sit at the gates of paradise could have made him happier. The divinity he had worshipped at a distance was now to be within daily approach. His instructions had been that he was to wait at the Princess's call. It grew pleasant to the girl to call him often. He came so gladly. And his services proved so helpful that, even after the recovery of Ferdinand, there remained a permanent friendship with the royal household. The young man never had known the love of a mother or a sister. The Crown Princess was the first woman he had ever come near.

So near did she feel him that she could now defy that loneliness which had so assailed her ever since her arrival in this Roumania. "A thousand faces and never a friend," she had been wont to think as she looked out on any public gathering, all of whom she said to herself were "people who had people that cared." Now for her too in this which had been so foreign a land, there was some one who cared. These, you see, were just two lonely young things who had found each other.

But one of them lived in a palace. Now a royal

court is a place that's like a glass house, with the
occupants living on a stage where footlights glare
night and day, and all the world is the audience
that watches. Even when it does not throw stones,
there is no move in the royal drama that escapes
public scrutiny. Residents of the court themselves,
limited to this little stage that surrounds a throne,
have as narrow a radius of expression as any country villager. So that an ingrown interest in each
other's affairs may develop an uncomfortable aspect. The Queen has told me that living in a
palace is like living in a house that has a hundred
rooms with never a key. And I know that as we
walked in the garden together, we might not so
much as step along a gravel path to smell of the
mignonette, without swift rumor flying ever ahead
of our coming that we had been there. Not a
whispering gallery itself affords less privacy than
a royal palace. The echo of a sigh or a kiss—Oh,
especially of a kiss—sounds as if it had been publicly megaphoned. With things this way, it is easy
to see how intrigue must flourish. There has
never, I suppose, been any royal court without
it. Smiling faces always all around. Always
smiling. But one may smile and smile and be a
gossip.

Well—but how was a girl of nineteen or twenty
or so to know! At the Cotroceni palace now there
were many parties. The old monastery walls rang
out with young people's gay laughter. The young
lieutenant was a born cotillion leader and the

Crown Princess danced like a nymph. In the orchestra that played were gypsy musicians who can make a violin sing with sweetness long drawn out. To the strains of the Blue Danube and the Vienna Waltz, two together whirled away into a world of dreams. And of course they rode together. Beatrice, "Baby B," came to visit her sister and then all three went walking in the forest. But Beatrice went home. And two walked in the forest alone.

Oh, with a whole court and all the world looking on! And Carmen Sylva so cold toward a girl to whom she must one day yield her own place. So what would happen, did happen. And a nursery governess of Carmen Sylva's appointing had helped to bring it about. It was afterward recalled that always she had been inquiring, Where has the Crown Princess gone to-day?

To King Carol they had brought the carefully accumulated story. And to his office Missy was summoned. She came before him. She stood again facing the massive table with the carved crouching lions beneath. The King was stern. Of course he had to be. Still somehow the girl got the impression that in some indefinable way "Uncle" was on her side. Perhaps he thought he ought to be, with so many against her.

But he hardened his voice when he spoke. It was particularly imperative, he pointed out, that a Crown Princess should not compromise herself. "We of course all know," he went on, "that Nanda may not be so very entertaining. But that does not mean that you may find your entertainment elsewhere." He concluded with a command that was also a statement: "There would be," he said, "no more walks in the forest, no more riding, no more dancing with the dark-eyed lieutenant." For the young man had already been banished to a foreign land.

It was long later that the lieutenant came back. He and the Honorary Colonel of the regiment reviewing her troops met just once face to face on the parade ground. There was only an eyelid's lifted glance along with the salute. Then they went on their way down the future, she to her crowning and he to a generalship in the Roumanian army.

That day from Uncle's office, Missy had gone straight to her husband. Frankly and fearlessly as was always her way, she announced: "Nanda, it seems all the court is talking. Soon they'll be talking to you. Only I'm going to talk first. It's quite true what they'll tell you, that Lieutenant —— loves me. He has said so. We have walked in the forest together. That much is true—but no more."

Nevertheless, the court hummed with the scandal. The Crown Princess demanded the dismissal of the spying governess. It was not done. So she packed instead and went home to her mother in Coburg. Weeks went by, strained, unhappy weeks. Queen Victoria had written old King

Carol: Wouldn't he do what he could to straighten out matters for the child? Probably he would have done so, had not events done it instead. The tide was turned when a telegram came to Coburg. It was from Nanda: Little Carol was very ill. Not all the court scandal and all the court intrigues could keep a mother from her child. As fast as the Orient express could carry her, the Crown Princess rushed back to her baby.

At the nursery door stood the governess who had spied: "It would be dangerous," the woman insisted, "to admit anyone to the baby's bedside. The doctor's instruction——"

But a voice interrupted: "Stand aside." Then, even more peremptorily: "The Crown Princess is the child's mother." And the voice was the voice of Nanda, but without hesitation, firm with authority. It mattered not what Uncle or Auntie or anyone else might say.

And there, by the bedside of their little son who was ill, two who had been estranged clasped hands again.

CHAPTER VII

Her Woman's Job

ONE must have children," says the Queen of Roumania. "It's a woman's job. Besides, I love them so." She has had six. It was a few months before the birth of the third that she found herself tiring too easily, when she attempted her customary walks in the forest. "Nana" she exclaimed to the devoted nurse in charge of her children, "do you know, it's a bother this having babies! And you have so much the best of me. For you have only the pleasure of loving my children, while me, I first have to bear them that I may have them to love." Once the Duchess of Edinburgh said to her daughter: "You love them best when they are little." "No," protested Marie, "I only seem to. Because that's the time they have such screaming need of me. But I love them just the same and just as much all along."

Missy was still wearing her hair in a braid turned up and tied with a ribbon behind, when her first baby came to her arms. And her second. She was, to be sure, only a child herself. And those about her quite failed to understand her joyous outlook on life. Frivolous, was what they thought her. "You see," she explains to-day, "I never could look too hard at things. If I did, it always made me cry. They never knew the sob I smothered in my throat."

Well, the whole attitude of the court seemed to be to ignore the girl mother's right to her children: they appeared to belong to the country. Anyhow she was much too young to direct their upbringing, Uncle and Auntie decided. So they would do it for her. In that way it came about that the supervision of Carol and Elizabeta in their early, most important determining years, was largely taken out of the hands of their mother. Elizabeta was named for Auntie, as Carol had been for Uncle.

Carol, blue-eyed and golden-haired like his mother, as he is to this day, was a very lovely child. And it should be remembered that he was the idol of a kingdom, the first royal prince ever to have been born to Roumania. Everybody was interested in him. He was just as sunny and sweet of nature as of face. He was so always amenable to suggestion, agreeing easily with the wishes of those around him, so that he never gave anyone the least trouble. When he and Elizabeta were little things, toddling about hand in hand, there was a great difference in the two. As he was yielding and agreeable, she was forceful and assertive, not nearly so easy to handle, it was at an early age discovered. And as she grew up, she became probably the most difficult of all the royal children to manage. Elizabeta can make up her mind with a resolute determination that has never been easy to swerve from its course. When these children were very little, people observing the two sometimes commented: "A pity the little girl had not been the boy."

After Elizabeta, it was five years before the arrival of Marie who was named for her mother. Mignon, they have always called her. She too is fair and golden like the Queen, though not the least like her in personality. Mignon was the baby who came in that year when the strained relations of the young Crown Princess at the Roumanian court had reached the climax, which as with many another young wife had sent her home to mother. Though she had returned, she and Auntie still faced each other across a great divide. "While I was carrying Mignon," says the Queen, "there never was a night I did not go crying to bed. Yet by some divine miracle, Mignon was born a smiling child. She was always the sunshine of life in our household. I never so much as saw that child ever wrinkle her face to cry."

The first three children had been given names from the royal family. The next two were christened with the names of saints, which is a very customary practice in Roumania. Nikolai was born in 1903. Of him the Queen says: "Nicky I had because I made up my mind to have him. I decided I'd have another boy. And he is what was sent." Of all the children, Nikolai looks most like the King. He has fair hair and his mother's eyes. But still the contour of face and figure are his father all over again. He looks exactly as old photographs show Ferdinand to have looked at his age.

Ileana came along in 1908. They gave her the old Roumanian name that makes her seem more than all the rest a real Roumanian princess. She has very dark eyebrows and eyes that flash sometimes gray and sometimes dark blue beneath long silken dark lashes. She has too darker hair than the rest of the children. But she it is who has inherited in full measure her mother's vivid personality and charm. It seems to me that Ileana of all her children is the one that the Queen loves best. Though perhaps it is only that she loves her differently. "Mignon," the Queen said to me, "is the child of my body. I should know and sympathize if ever she had so much as an ache or a pain in her little finger. But Ileana is the child of my soul. I can just lay my hand on hers, and I know all that she is thinking. Again and again I have done it: 'You are thinking this or that, Ileana,' I say. And always it is so."

Mircaea, the last of the children, is the little boy who came to stay so short a time and went away again. Born December 21, 1912, he died during the war, October 20th, 1916. They had named him after one of the heroes of early Roumanian history. Her Majesty sleeps always with Mircaea's last little shoes in an embroidered case beneath her pillow. Tenderly she unfolded the case to show me: "See how stubby they are," she pointed out. "You know, I love them to look like that. For he was such a stubborn, naughty little boy. I see him still kissing Ileana's dolls goodnight as they lay four in a row. But I like best to remember him as he was when he'd run away with his rattling little red cart right out into the middle of the road." The Queen put carefully away again the little worn shoes shaped by the sturdy baby feet that never more would run away. "Who shall say what Mircaea might have grown up to be!" she mused.

The royal children were always in the charge of English nurses. Up in England at Windsor on Clewer Road stands a little red brick cottage with "Mignon Villa" inscribed over the front door. Mary Green retired, lives there. And she has named her cottage, you see, for what she calls her "last baby." Mary Green was the first nurse for the Queen's children. Carol and Elizabeta and Mignon she started in life, and by that time she was no longer young. Then she herself it was who suggested her successor, Ellen Woodfield, to have charge of Nicky and Ileana and Mircaea as they came along. Now Miss Woodfield still stays on in the royal household, which is probably her permanent home. Against the colorful background of the Roumanian court, she is a striking, dignified, and wholly Anglo-Saxon little figure. She wears her white hair parted and waved softly

away from her face. She is little and gentle and
fragile like a flower. The edelweiss I always
thought of when I looked at Ellen Woodfield. It
is difficult to realize that she ever could have sat
a young prince down hard on a chair in a corner.
But she did. And he sat until she told him he
might get up. Nicky knows. And everybody else
says how excellent was her discipline. Now that
the nursery no longer needs Ellen Woodfield, the
whole household seems to. A lady-in-waiting
wants a string to tie a package for the mail, and it
is Miss Woodfield who gets it. Ileana, starting on
a journey, has at the last moment lost the keys
to her trunks. And it is Miss Woodfield, "Ninnie," as all the children still call her, who finds
the trunk man and gets the new keys just in time
for the princess to catch the departing train.
Nikolai, home from Eton, went always first to his
mother and then to Ninnie to "tell her all about
it." Even the Queen herself likes to have Ninnie
around; and you see them working often side by
side in the garden.

Her Majesty's capacity for warm human friendship knows no limitation of class. To the nurses
to whom she committed her children's welfare
she kept always very near. And then it was her
custom to leave to their judgment the daily details of the little princes' and princesses' existence.
In that way was developed a responsibility and a
pride that contributed largely to the efficiency of
the royal nursery. When the Queen was yet a

young Crown Princess, her mother the Duchess
had advised: "In your situation there can be no
two ways about it. You cannot personally attend
to every want of your children from bodily to spiritual needs. You cannot possibly do this and at the
same time meet all the social obligations sure to
be increasingly imposed by your royal position.
So the only sensible course for you is to put in
charge of your nursery a competent person whom
you can trust. Then let her run it."

So first "Nana" and then "Ninnie," as the babies
called them, had very general supervision of the
royal children from their diet to their dress, and
until they passed on to governesses and tutors, even
to their deportment. All of them speak fluently
three languages, their native Roumanian and English, and of course also French. People often have
commented on their perfect English. "Well, why
shouldn't it be perfect? I taught them," says Ellen
Woodfield. They have all been brought up in the
Greek Orthodox Church, the requirements of
which faith they carefully observe. Over each
child's bed hung always the ikon that is the picture
of his or her particular patron saint. But always
also at twilight they were gathered together to sing
softly that very old hymn, "Gentle Jesus meek and
mild." And at the knees of Anglo-Saxon nurses,
they repeated straight to God the very simple
little prayer their mother taught them. Each child
has always said it: "O dear God, bless and guard
all those that I love: Papa and Mama, Grand-

mamma, Uncle and Auntie, my brothers and sisters, and all kind friends. And make me a good and obedient child. For Jesus' sake, Amen." Even to the years of their later growing up, Ninnie never ceased to stress for her charges the importance of the habit of spiritual contact. Ileana, a big girl and going to parties, sometimes has come home at night so weary with gaiety that she has dropped forgetfully into bed. "But, dearie," remonstrates Ninnie, "you haven't said your prayers." "Going to say them in bed," sleepily pleads the tired girl. "It won't be at all the same," firmly insists Ninnie. Nothing like that will do. So a young princess in her white nightgown must slide out of bed to go down to her knees as usual in prayer to God.

It was of course Nurse Green who did the pioneer work in establishing and organizing the royal nursery. No less a personage than Grandmamma the Queen had selected her and sent her down to Roumania to Missy's assistance at the time when Uncle and Auntie were presuming to assume too much authority in the guardianship of those first babies. Mary Green was already attached to the English royal family by long tenure of service. Her grandmother had been a maid in Queen Victoria's household. She herself had been the nurse for the children of Victoria's daughter, Princess Christine. And as these children were taken often together with those of the Duke of Edinburgh to play in the park, Mary Green of course knew in their little girlhood Missy and Ducky and Sandra. Now she came very gladly to do for Missy's babies in turn.

Upon Queen Victoria's insistence she had been at the birth of Carol installed in charge of the nursery. And sometimes there were clashes with the eastern environment. There had been a wet nurse secured for the baby. And Mary Green on her arrival found this young woman taking her meals with the rest of the servants over at great Castle Pelash. That would never do. Suppose something in her diet should disagree with the baby. "I must have her eat right here under my supervision," Nurse Green declared to the young father. "But," replied Ferdinand, "it will never be possible to get Uncle to change a program he has already made." "We'll have to see about that," answered Mary Green. The next time the old King visited the nursery to inquire about the future heir to the kingdom, she replied laconically: "Well, Your Majesty, so far the little prince is still all right. But," she added grimly, "I really cannot guarantee his health for the future unless I can have different arrangements." She got them. And gradually she had the nursery staff pretty well under her control.

Only whenever there was a question of a difference in methods, it was the Roumanian way that everybody around considered superior to the English. The doctors, Mary Green usually had to stand aside for. But there was the time Carol had the croup. She had begged that they treat him the English way. But, no, they wouldn't. And he was a very sick child. At last all the specialists could only announce that the baby was dying. "Come away, Missy darling," urged Ferdinand, his arm about his young wife's waist. "There is nothing more we can do here. Only we can pray."

"Well, then," announced Nurse Green when they had all given up the case, "there's something I can do if I'm allowed." She looked at the Crown Prince. He nodded his permission. In a few minutes she had plunged the baby in a hot bath. Then she gave him an emetic. In an hour the crisis had passed; the baby was sleeping naturally.

To the young mother in those early years of adjustment, Nurse Green was probably the greatest comfort east of the Carpathians. That time the young Crown Princess went home to Coburg, it was with Mary Green she left her babies, Carol, six and Elizabeta, five. After her departure, Carmen Sylva countermanded some of the nursery arrangements and Nurse Green sturdily resisted so long as that was possible. But they insisted that the younger child Elizabeta required all her care. So Carol was separated from her, to be left much in charge of the nursery governess whose meddling in court affairs had made so much trouble for Missy. And the influences about the child were not tending for his best development. Almost fortunately, it seems, he fell ill with that attack of typhoid which opened the way for his mother's return. As the little boy began to get better, it was discovered that during her absence someone had undertaken to revise his bedtime devotions. He was found to be saying a prayer in which the "God bless Mamma" had been carefully cut from the category of all of the rest of the family who were placed under divine protection. Of course that was at once corrected. And soon Mary Green was again established in the nursery.

Now the third baby's advent was expected. But the Roumanian court did not yet afford the most harmonious atmosphere. It was not only that Carmen Sylva assumed almost a critical, dictatorial, mother-in-law attitude. It should be remembered also that she was considered to be something of a genius. Certainly she had a temperamental endowment which made her more or less subject to moods. So the Duchess of Edinburgh wrote, urging that Missy come to Coburg-Gotha for the approaching confinement. And the young wife, too, felt that this would be best. This time however, she would take her nursery with her. Mary Green and Carol and Elizabeta all went along, the Crown Prince himself accompanying them.

Preparations for departure and for the coming event were under way at Cotroceni. The lovely layette that was being collected was laid out piece by piece in a room reserved for that purpose, the door being kept carefully locked. The Crown

Princess and Mary Green were both engaged in this assembling. So that several times now the children had been sent with one of the nursemaids for their afternoon walk. No, Nana could not go, she replied to their expostulations. Why couldn't she go? Oh, because she was busy. Now run along.

One of these afternoon walks, because of a sudden shower, had terminated earlier than was anticipated. And the door to the interesting room stood still ajar. Suddenly Nurse Green, looking up from a pile of little things in her arms, saw Elizabeta staring at proceedings from the threshold. "I guess I know what all this means," said the child wisely. "It seems to me there's going to be a baby at our house."

Thus challenged, astonished nurse Green replied: "Well, I think perhaps. But if God is to send one, you'll have to be very good. Above all, you mustn't mention the matter to anyone but your mother."

Elizabeta nodded. But it would be hard about father. She especially liked to share things with father. However, this he must not know. She decided she had to keep her promise. Otherwise, God might change all the plans. To her mother alone she confided the great secret that a baby would be coming soon.

In the old palace at Gotha, no child had been born for more than a hundred years. Such an event was awaited therefore with interest. The nursery which had been opened for Carol and

Elizabeta was in a remote wing. And as her time approached, it had not been possible for their mother to come to them every day. Then one night very late, there was a soft step in the nursery. An electric light was suddenly switched on. Nurse Green, occupying a bed between her two small charges, sat up in alarm. But she caught the gleam of a diamond diadem: "Hush," said the Crown Princess, raising a warning finger. Just as she was, she had come from the opera. "Hush," she repeated. "I didn't mean to startle you, Nana. But I wanted one glimpse of the darlings to-night. For I feel that I may not be coming to see them again now for some time." It was just midnight when the Crown Princess went out in her diadem and her shimmering evening gown. At one o'clock, the personal maid of the Duchess came to the nursery to announce, "The party's begun." "Then," said Nana "I might just as well get up. Because they are sure to be wanting me." Well, they did. But by three o'clock, it was all over. By four o'clock, everybody was sitting down to breakfast.

When all the rush had subsided, Ferdinand suggested, "Nana, you better tell Elizabeta and Carol they have a new baby sister." "No," objected Nurse Green, "Your Royal Highness better tell them yourself." Soon Ferdinand came back, holding both his sides with laughter: "Nana," he exclaimed, "What do you suppose that remarkable child Elizabeta said to me? She just looked at me without the least surprise, 'Why Papa,' she said, 'I knew all about that long ago.' "

The new baby was of course engaging every one's attention. Everyone was making pleasant remarks. But the young father, gazing critically down at the red crumpled face of his new little daughter, complained, "She's not what I call good looking." "That'll come later," interposed Nurse Green.

It was three months afterward that the Crown Prince had come again to Coburg to gather up his family for the homeward trip to Roumania. Nana stepped forward eagerly to present her small charge. "That my child?" exclaimed Ferdinand in amazement. "Sure, it's none other," affirmed Nurse Green. "But she's so good looking," declared the happy father. "Didn't I say she would be?" triumphantly retorted Mary Green.

On the return to Cotroceni, the Crown Princess as she grew older, was able more and more to assert her personality. Still the old King and Queen never quite relinquished their control of Carol and Elizabeta. A new nursery governess had replaced the one whom Missy had found so objectionable. King Carol considered her specially qualified because of previous service in the household of the Queen of Holland. No one however had thought to consult Missy about that appointment. Nor had she any decision in the choice of a tutor for Carol. As a matter of fact, she never was satisfied with the Swiss German

tutor whom they selected. Nor with the program
at Potsdam where Carol was sent for his military
training.

Of course, all the while the children were growing up, there were minor matters that might have
made discord. But Missy's sense of humor now
usually saved the situation and smoothed her path.
She particularly desired that her children be
simply dressed. "Let it be serge or some nice
wash material," she would frequently recommend
as she and Nana together talked over the question
of clothes. Then, often she would add, "But Nana,
I leave it to you. You know what I want. Only
let everything be quite practical and sensible."

It was Auntie who had very much more elaborate ideas about how the children should be dressed.
Once she got Carol into a little Lord Fauntleroy
suit, which in those days was considered quite
elegant. When by chance the Crown Princess
heard in advance what was coming, she sent Nana
in haste to the shop where the suit was being made.
"What color has been ordered for the little Prince
Carol's suit?" inquired Nurse Green. "Blue, was
what Her Majesty Queen Elizabeth said," the
shop assistant replied. "Then the Crown Princess
sends word, 'Let it be dark blue,'" Nurse Green
instructed. And it was that quiet color. Which
was of course some relief.

Marie never could endure to have her children
dolled up and fussed up. She especially
disliked that they be in any way conspicu-

ous. And Auntie had the habit of presenting to them articles of dress inclined to be violently German in taste. At the time of the silver wedding anniversary of the Duke and the Duchess of Coburg, all the Cotroceni family were making ready to attend. "I'll get Elizabeta's outfit," offered Carmen Sylva. "But we've got nearly everything already," hastily rejoined Marie. "Then I'll get a pelisse and a hat for the child," cheerfully insisted Auntie.

And later, one afternoon, Nana appeared to announce, "It's come, Your Royal Highness." "Is it perfectly dreadful, yellow or some awful color like that?" inquired the anxious young mother. "I think it's even worse than yellow," was Nana's lugubrious admission. She opened the box, to display a very brilliant pink, pink, little coat and hat. Marie covered her face with her hands to shut out the blaze of color.

"But it's good ribbed silk and the white ostrich feather is quite all right," comforted Nana. "Well," affirmed the Crown Princess with decision, "we'll not take the things to Coburg with us anyhow. Of course the child will have to wear them here in Bucharest for Auntie to see. But never, never put them on when she's going out with me."

Then the Crown Princess and Mary Green both laughed when the latter recalled the story about Grandmamma the Queen. In Missy's own little girlhood, Victoria always was presenting to her

158

grandchildren Scotch kilts for the little boys and
Tartan plaid sashes for the little girls. And it did
not matter at all whether the little girls happened
to be dark or light or how the kilts looked on any
particular little boy. Everyone had to wear these
gifts just the same, because they had come from
Grandmamma the Queen. After all, one generation follows another with a repetition of much
the same situation in human relations.

In due course of time the Crown Princess had
secured more and more control of her nursery.
And to this end Mary Green's faithful coöperation had contributed not a little. So completely
harmonious had been the relations with her royal
mistress, that, as Nurse Green likes to tell you to-
day: "Her Royal Highness never said to me an
unkind word in all the time I was in her service.
Some would have been jealous about the children.
She wasn't, even though they always howled if
I left their sight. She just seemed glad to have
them love me so. The nearest she ever came to
speaking severely to me was when once we had
come to a little difference of opinion about some
of the children's clothes: 'Now, Nana,' exclaimed
the Crown Princess, 'I'm cross. You'd better
go!'"

"So I did," says Nurse Green. "I just gathered up my baby in my arms and made for the
nursery." Even the old King Carol himself paid
his tribute to Mary Green's tact and skill. He
had come to say good-by as she was resigning her

place to her successor. Taking both her hands in his, he said: "We haven't always quite agreed. But I know very well now how much we all owe to you." And there were tears in his eyes.

For the bringing up of her younger children, it came about at last that the Crown Princess had free scope to apply her own ideas. It has from the first been one of her fundamental policies that children be permitted to grow in the way that God intended for the particular personality of each. Ileana, spontaneous, responsive, vivacious, one of the most delightful and engaging young girls that one may meet, might not have been like that to-day if she had been repressed in her childhood. She was one of those children with a boundless capacity for imagination, the kind that in past times used to get spanked for telling fibs, and that way sometimes robbed of their natural birthright for seeing visions. Once Ileana had returned from a visit with Ninnie to a school, the first school she had ever seen. She narrated to her mother such an interesting account of it all that the Queen later repeated some of the amazing details. Ninnie listened, at first mystified. Then she turned to her young charge to admonish in shocked tones: "Ileana, I'm afraid you have been again telling your mother something which is not so."

"Was it true, dear? Was it really true?" then asked the Queen. The child looked up thoughtfully and answered: "Well, maybe not really, you

MARIE IN HER CORONATION ROBES

MRS. DAGGETT AT THE ENTRANCE TO CASTLE
BRAN WEARING THE ROUMANIAN PEASANT
COSTUME LOANED HER BY THE QUEEN

THE QUEEN AND MRS. DAGGETT IN THE COURT-
YARD OF CASTLE BRAN

BRAN, THE FAIRY-TALE CASTLE OF THE QUEEN

THE QUEEN BESIDE THE LAKE IN THE GARDEN
AT BRAN

THE DUKE AND DUCHESS OF EDINBURGH WITH
THEIR FOUR DAUGHTERS. GEORGE, THE PRESENT
KING OF ENGLAND, STANDS BEHIND MISSY WHO
IS HOLDING ROSES.

THE QUEEN BEFORE AN OLD
ROUMANIAN CROSS

THE QUEEN IN NATIVE PEASANT DRESS

THE CROWN PRINCESS MARIE AT THIRTY

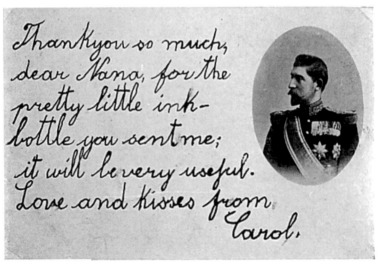

Thank you so much,
dear Nana, for the
pretty little ink-
bottle you sent me;
it will be very useful.
Love and kisses from
Carol.

A LETTER FROM THE LITTLE CAROL TO HIS NURSE
ON A PICTURE POSTCARD OF FERDINAND

MRS. DAGGETT AT THE ENTRANCE OF COTROCENI PALACE

THE HONORARY COLONEL OF THE REGIMENT

MIGNON, QUEEN OF SERBIA, WITH HER
MOTHER AND HER SON

ELIZABETA WHO MARRIED THE KING
OF GREECE

THE QUEEN WITH MIRCAEA,
THE CHILD WHO DIED

KING FERDINAND

THE QUEEN WITH ILEANA

PRINCE NICHOLAS

PRINCESS ILEANA

THE QUEEN WITH HER GRANDSON MIHAI, HEIR
APPARENT TO THE THRONE

LITTLE PRINCE MIHAI

MIHAI WITH HIS MOTHER, THE GREEK PRINCESS HELENE

MIHAI WITH HIS FATHER, EX-CROWN PRINCE CAROL

know. But then," she added brightly, "you see, mother, it might have been." The Queen nodded. Yes, she could see. Then once again, very carefully, she went over with the child the difference between fact and fiction. But never did she ruthlessly curb that divine gift which had endowed Ileana to see all through life the magical might-have-been. Always the child was kept quite unafraid and absolutely natural.

This was a quality that contributed to Ileana's charm as even a very small girl. When she was seven, she was visiting with her mother at Buckingham Palace. And the King of England was enchanted with her. Perhaps it was that Ileana reminded him of another little girl, a golden-haired little girl in the days when he was young.

"Why do you eat so many bananas?" asked the King one day. "Because we had none at all at Jassy," answered the child. "What did you do at Jassy?" inquired the King. "Carried thermos bottles of hot tea, just as Mamma did, to the soldiers who lay freezing and dying in the streets," replied Ileana. But she went busily on eating bananas. The sweets passed. And the cheese passed. She would have none of them. "Will you never have had enough bananas?" asked the King. "Never," said the child, "I think, while you have any left."

It was on the occasion of this same visit at Buckingham Palace that Admiral Sims from America was present one day as a luncheon guest. He was waiting in the drawing-room. And Ileana was discovered there entertaining the gentleman. They had already become so well acquainted that the Admiral had asked, "Won't you give me a kiss?"

"Why, yes, certainly," responded the child with composure, "if you want it." The Prince of Wales now had entered the room. "Can I have one, too?" asked the young man.

"Of course," came the cheerful response. And then as she looked him over, "I'd like it myself." Later, recounting the incident to her mother, Ileana concluded, "I liked best to kiss the Prince."

Nikolai, too, like Ileana, has been brought up to be all that is himself. And he has that same spirit of spontaneity that so easily makes friends. Somehow whenever Nicky is around, you seem to sense, as it were, something like a fresh breeze on a summer's day. A telegram laid by the Queen's plate at luncheon, where I sat beside her, was from Nicky. He would be coming home, it said, on furlough from the English navy. This was only the first bulletin. Nicky was travelling all the way from London with his own car and without a chauffeur. For two days the household was kept in a state of excitement with arriving telegrams that told of his progress: "Now I am at Dijon;" "Now I am at Montenegro;" and so on the telegraph wires reported. Finally, at dinner on Thursday evening, word was received that Nicky had crossed the Roumanian frontier. In the middle of the night, he made his sensational entry through the castle gates. He was a little late at breakfast the next morning. But we all moved along to make a place for him beside the Queen. He kissed his mother and she said: "I'm glad to see you so clean and in such good order so early in the morning. There are sausages," she added.

"Good," exclaimed her son. "I've been dreaming about them." "Now tell me all about yourself," went on the Queen. So Nicky described in detail his trip and the roads and then his ship. "How about your captain? Do you like him?" inquired the Queen.

"Well," said Nicky, a trifle dubiously, "his name's Dashwood. We call him Crashwood. In the morning he's fairly yellow, he's so sour."

"But how often have I taught you," admonished the Queen, "that the morning with some people is a difficult hour. Never in the morning ask anything of anyone, except your mother."

It had been, the Queen explained to me, something of a feat in these democratic times to have secured for a foreign Prince a berth in another navy. Nicky protested: "Why, for a smile from you, Ma'am, I could have been made Admiral of the British Navy." And he leaned forward to offer his mother a light for her cigarette.

Nicky, I think, is one of the most satisfactory of her children. His education has been just as she desired it. He went, you remember, to Eton because she so cleverly maneuvered it. He made

163

no brilliant record. But he was always good at
mathematics. He always liked machinery, especially an automobile, better than books. He certainly wasn't as keen for hard study as some would
have wished. "Never mind," decided his mother.
"Who really learns so very much from books, anyhow? Nicky doesn't need to learn from books if
he learns from life. What if he doesn't read at
all? Perhaps he will later. Anyhow, I'm not going to curb him too much. I believe in giving him
his head. More than all my children, he has the
joy of life. And I won't spoil it."

The wider contact she had secured for Nikolai
by sending him away to school the Queen considered as good for daughters as for sons. Elizabeta's training, according to the wishes of Uncle
and Auntie, had been with governesses at home.
Well, there were these, too, for the younger daughters. But the Queen deemed it also essential that
they have the experience of daily living with other
girls. So Mignon and then Ileana were sent in
turn to a well known English school at Heath-
field, Ascot, near Eton, where Nicky went. And
all of them were not far from that little Villa
Mignon at Windsor. This was reckoned a particular advantage. In the event of homesickness,
Nana would be always near.

Few of their royal relatives to this day are as
close to these children, and even to the Queen
herself, as is this old family nurse. Mary Green's
connection with the royal household was never

really severed. Always she used to meet the family for the vacations spent at Coburg, and for other special occasions she was ever on call. All of the royal sons and daughters she counts as "her children." The arrival of each new baby who came after her departure from Cotroceni was always telegraphed to her. She has every baby picture, every little girl and boy picture ever taken of all the princes and princesses. Now the wedding pictures, too, have been coming alone. And the walls of Villa Mignon, like a gallery, are literally covered with royal family photographs.

There is no joy or grief that has come to these, her darlings, in which Mary Green has not shared. It is now more than twenty years since she left active nursery service. Yet for all this time, save for interruptions due to difficulties of communication during the war, there has come from Her Majesty a weekly letter with full friendly news of all the family. Here are a few of these letters selected at random. Read:

Cotroceni, April 14, 1916.

DEAR NANA: The children are all well and a great pleasure to me, each in their own way. Perhaps Ileana is the most perfect of all. She is lovely, good, and intelligent, and quite adorable with her obstinate little brother. Lisabetta sings very prettily, has a nice talent for drawing. She is very beautiful. Carol is a great worker and a good boy, gives us no trouble as some sons do. Mignon is as good as she promised to become as a baby. Nikolai is intelligent, excitable, energetic, the funniest and most witty of all. And Mircaea, the baby, is an obstinate slow delightful little creature who will talk only Roumanian and whom I love with all my heart. What times we are living in! Will it ever end? And what is our fate to be? Well, it is no good pondering and making one's self miserable before hand. One must just have the courage to face every fate. Well, Good-by for to-day. All the children send you their love. The King is well and very nice. The family circle is a very happy one. MARIE.

Cotroceni, August 15, 1916.

MY DEAR OLD NANA: You must be lonely and isolated in these bad moments of horrible war. It never seems to come to an end. Now we are half through the summer and an anxious summer, as the war is very near us and the danger is never excluded that we will be drawn into it one way or another. As to health we are, thank God, all well from the big ones to the little ones. Carol has become a very busy man and a good soldier. He has also organized boy scouts through all the country. He is a hard worker and knows how to carry things through. Lisabetta is very beautiful. Mignon is as good, easy, and sweet as she was when you had her in your arms. Nicky is very amusing and clever. He is the one that makes us all laugh. My Ileana is the one who has irreproachable manners. She is naturally amiable and utterly sweet, an extraordinarily perfect child. Mircaea is rather naughty and very delicious. The King is well, but has too many worries. My life is very busy. . . .

Cotroceni, December 3, 1918.

DEAR NANA: I suppose you have heard that Carol gave us much trouble. But I still hope to save him. He had always been such a good obedient boy. But, alas, he fell into bad hands as often happens to very good boys. . . .

Cotroceni, May 14, 1921.

MY DEAR OLD NANA: These have been busy times for me. Thank God, my two children are now happily married and I am very satisfied about it all. I left Lisabetta in what I think looks like a very happy home with a first-rate man who loves her deeply and whom she is learning to love. Carol arrived a week ago with his sweet young wife. We love her. She is pretty and good and kind. . . .

Cotroceni, March 16, 1922.

DEAR OLD NANA: Here we are all well and preparing for Mignon's wedding, which is to be at Belgrade June 1. Both the King and I dread her departure more than we can say. For Lisabetta we wished marriage. She was getting restless at home. But Mignon is gloriously happy with us and fills the house with good cheer and sunshine. Nicky finished Eton this year. So we shall have him home soon after Mignon leaves, which will be a blessing. We dread the house emptying. Ileana is growing so big. I am always sad to see them grow up. . . .

Sinaia, August 19, 1922.

DEAR OLD NANA: Thank you in Mignon's name for the dear little book you sent her for her wedding. Here is a photograph of her in her wedding dress with the beautiful emeralds Alexander gave her. She was a sweet bride and now we have the happiest news about her. Lisabetta has at last arrived here after her terrible illness. She is still very weak, but so happy to be home. Nicky must also arrive to-day, having finished his time at Eton. So the house is filling up again. . . .

Belgrade, Serbia, Sept. 22, '23.

DEAR OLD NANA: We safely received your letter but not your telegram. And both Mignon and I thank you heartily. She is getting on splendidly. Had what is called an easy confinement, if one can ever call such a thing easy. She is gloriously, radiantly happy with her tiny but extraordinarily contented baby. Her King is of course beaming with joy. And pride throughout the kingdom is great. Of course, I am full of gratitude that all went off so well. There my dear

167

child sits in her bed with her glorious fair hair about her face, lovingly smiling down upon her dark little baby. And somehow it all seems quite natural. . . .

Cotroceni, October 3, 1923.

DEAR OLD NANA: How are you? And how are the poor rheumatic knees getting along? Here everything goes well with us. The Princess, Carol's wife, is all that my heart could desire. And Ileana is growing up sweet and beautiful. After many storms and much trouble, I am happy in my children. Pray God, Nana, to keep me so. MARIE.

Well, see how through all the letters to Nana, the years are ringing their changes. But her woman's job as a mother, goes steadily on for the Queen. Those who as little things had such "screaming" need of her, seem only to develop new demands as the birthdays go by. Comes play, comes schooling, comes love making, comes marriage. And each succeeding epoch presents its own complications.

Now see how marriage engages the attention of the Queen of Roumania. Kings have sought her daughters. For several years since, sovereigns, or those to be, entering the matrimonial lists, have cast a careful eye over the map of Europe and then paused speculatively at Roumania, even though it was "way down there." "Are there any more at home like her?" has been ever the thoughtful inquiry. You see it is the loveliness and the fame of a very beautiful mother, quite as much as their own qualifications, that have recommended for thrones the attractive Roumanian princesses.

Quite frankly, too, the Queen has wanted thrones for them. She believes in maintaining their class. "My daughters," she says, "belong to a special breed, a very special breed because it is a royal breed. Marriage is under the best of circumstances, difficult enough. Why complicate it then with a chasm of class across which two people will never be able really to find each other."

Now because of this limitation to class, there has always been a proverbial difficulty, true love never running smooth for royalty, you know. For as likely as not, it may run off the gravel path to take some more devious and even more interesting course. It is right here that the Queen sees required the exercise of motherhood's highest skill. There is no greater cruelty to a girl, she believes, than to permit for her an alliance outside her own kind. A girl when she's young doesn't know about that. But her elders know. And it's their duty to protect her future happiness.

But Marie of Roumania believes in love. Oh yes indeed, as the greatest thing in the world. Why, God is love. And real love, spiritual love between man and woman, is that which links them with the divine. She has wanted for her daughters no alliance without love. But she finds it just as easy for a girl to fall in love with the right man of her own class as with a wrong one outside it— if only the stage is set. You see, to almost any girl, a good looking young man by the river's brink is always a good looking young man, and nothing less. Well then, compose that picture into which you let your daughter step. Have your right young man waiting at the river's brink. Then, when along comes the maiden walking down the path where brook and river meet, that which is as inevitable as any other miracle of nature, will occur. But it's up to a mother to make it come true.

So the Queen's methods with her daughters have been to safeguard their environment. While the young officers whom they were meeting were all nice young men, a royal Princess must not be permitted to look too long in their eyes nor they in hers. Because these are not of a class with whom a girl like this could mate. Even in her own class, there are princes and princes. The Queen always has watched out lest even an undesirable prince play too long about a daughter of hers. Even if he's royal, she stipulates, he must not be cross-eyed, or bow-legged or stupid. When anything of that sort comes prowling around, she is instantly on the alert to remove a daughter to a safe distance. Oh, it is quite true that the Queen takes careful matrimonial forethought for her children. It is with intention that she has desired to marry them off advantageously from reasons of state. Yet she would not in any instance, she declares, promote a marriage not fraught with the greatest ultimate happiness for the child's concern.

"You see," says the Queen, "I know my children so well, and what is best for them. There was Elizabeta, very beautiful and with so many

suitors she could not make up her own mind. So
I quietly lent my influence to the most desirable
one." In 1922, Elizabeta was wedded to George
the Duke of Sparta, who later succeeded his
brother on the throne. And Elizabeta was a
Queen of Greece until that country became a re-
public. Then for Mignon also a king came a-
courting, King Alexander, ruler of the kingdom
of the Serbs, Croats, and Slovenes. "Now my
Mignon," the Queen says, "was always quiet and
retiring and the most unselfish of all my children.
But she was not in the least romantic. And I saw
this which was being offered as an excellent
destiny for Mignon. I explained to her that a
great and a good man wanted her for his wife to
make his home and to bear his children. More-
over, his country needed a queen for whom there
would be a great future in which to develop Serbia
even as I have Roumania. But, I added that it was
for her to decide whether or no she wished to accept this destiny. We waited a little, Ferdinand
and I. Then we told the King of Serbia we
thought the situation with Mignon favorable
enough so that he would not be risking a refusal.
He came. They were alone three hours. Then
Mignon came leading him by the hand. He could
not speak English. Mignon said: 'Mother, we
have arranged it'—and burst into tears. Yet to-day
my little Queen of Serbia is a happy woman. In
just nine months she had given her new country
an heir. She begins, you see, to follow in my foot-

steps. She did a woman's first duty and did it promptly and straight off. Now for her, the whole world centers in her baby Peter. Elizabeta, her sister, has as yet made no contribution to a future generation. Elizabeta, I fear, is more modern. It is my little Serbian Queen who preserves the traditions."

There remains the Princess Ileana whose Prince Charming is yet to appear. And I think he will have to be very charming. The King of Bulgaria has long been anxiously waiting. The heir to the throne of Italy sometime ago made approaches. The Prince of Wales, the most eligible of course of the royal scions of Europe, has said meditatively of Ileana, "She's a jolly little kid."

Meanwhile the Queen has declared, "I shall not marry Ileana even to a King, unless she loves him." At the same time and with equal firmness, she has announced that princes without thrones for Ileana to sit on, need not apply. A number of these, quite nice boys, too, the Queen has already told to run along. And they are not, she says, so easy to dispose of. There was one who stayed around so long that it was noticeable Ileana began to like to have him in the landscape. Then the Queen gently advised his family they'd better find him something to do. "You see," says the Queen, "no woman can love a man she can't look up to. He's got to be stronger than she. He's got to be taking his part in life. And if he's born to be a ruler, well then he's got to be ruling."

For sons as for daughters, the Queen has found that careful guidance is required. Between her and her Nikolai there exists the most delightful understanding. It is to his mother that Nicky has always come with his confidences about the latest girl and the love affair that this time is to be forever. He came at eighteen with the first one. There was visiting at the Roumanian court a young sister of that Greek Princess whom his elder brother, Carol, had married. And Nicky and the Princess Irene, also just eighteen, appeared before his mother one day, their arms about each other's waists: "We're in love," they announced.

"My children," exclaimed the Queen, "but you're young! You'll have to wait of course. All the same," and she smiled reassuringly, "I'll see what can be done, Nicky. I'll have to find the right moment to break it to your father."

Well, she did. And the King was agreeable. He thought Irene a very nice girl. But it was the Prime Minister who demurred.

"What would you have then?" demanded the Queen. "I think this marriage which the boy proposes would be a nice clean manly thing for him to do."

Still the Prime Minister insisted that King Constantine, the father of the young lady, was at that time a king who was down on his luck and with all the world against him. Roumania ought to require a princess in better standing.

"Well, who then?" the Queen demanded. And

she made him scan Europe with her. "You see how limited is the matrimonial market," she pointed out, "when you take into consideration religion and everything else; practically only one other royal princess is at all suitable for Nicky, and she's so much younger that the marriage must wait for years."

But the Prime Minister remained obdurate. So the Queen said: "O, very well then. But who knows what may happen to Nicky in the meantime? Suppose he arrives here at court one day, bringing some plain Miss Kate Jenkins for a bride. Or, these are days when the stage is ambitious; perhaps she'll be a variety actress. I'll do my best to hold Nicky. But of course I don't guarantee anything," the Queen concluded.

Then to the young people she announced: "My dears, there are difficulties in your path. The Roumanian government requires that a prince shall look around a little more before he decides on marriage. If you're really in love, it will last. If you've not got the real thing, this is an excellent opportunity for finding it out." So the Queen soothed the two young things. Time now seems to have effected its own adjustment. And as yet Nicky has staged no spectacular matrimonial event for the world to stare at.

But it is Carol who has set two continents to talking. Carol, the very good little boy. Carol, who as a young man in his teens, was still such a nice youth. He was always so sweet with the

younger children: why, when the last baby was
born, Carol loved him so that if little Mircaea
cried at night, he'd walk the floor with him like
a father. Carol was always so dependable and so
dear. See by the Queen's letters to Nana. Right
up to the time of the trouble, he was a model
obedient son.

Then the crash came. Who shall say how?
You can't just say it was "Zizi." Carol married
her, Jeanne Lambrino, in 1918, without benefit
of anybody's permission. She was the daughter
of a General and came from an old Roumanian
family. But of course she wasn't royal. It was
a runaway match when everybody was busy with
the war. They had gone by automobile to Odessa
in Russia, where they were married by the rites of
their own Greek religion. But they were appre-
hended and brought back. Carol was even imprisoned on the charge of desertion from his regiment. Eventually the marriage was annulled. It
was that old recurring motif that crops out so
regularly somewhere in almost every generation
of every royal house, love beyond the confines of
the royal code. Nothing can be more forbidden.

But perhaps that had been so taken for granted,
that in all the course of Carol's growing up nobody had remembered to stress sufficiently the
fundamental tenet of all the royalist creed: that
the heir to a throne must place the demands of his
country above his personal desires, even the dearest
personal desire of his own heart. And it was

Uncle's and Auntie's doing that little Carol was always being impressed with how much was going to be his when he should become a man. When he was five and Elizabeta four, they were walking hand in hand at Sinaia one day. There were carpenters at work on great Castle Pelash. The children noticed that repairs were being made. And doubtless their comment, as with other children, more or less reflected the conversation of their elders at Castle Pelasor. "Now what do you suppose they are doing up there?" asked Elizabeta critically. "Putting on a new roof to Uncle's house," answered Carol. "Umph," returned Elizabeta, "might better add a new room to our house." "No," said Carol. "I'm glad Uncle is making his castle nicer, because some day it will be my castle." Always the ideal that was crystallizing in the child's mind was that one day he would possess the kingdom, not that he would inherit an obligation to serve his country.

Then he came along at last to the age at which a great many boys would give a kingdom for a girl. And Carol thought he had one to give. Always he had been so good and obedient, yielding readily to the influence of those about him. Well now, here was a new influence, a perfect magnet of influence, Zizi with all the insistent call of her bright youth. "Take the throne," he cried, counting everything well lost for love. "Give me the girl."

But it was then Carol found a royal inheritance is a thing heavily mortgaged with obligations, and

not to be lightly traded and disposed of. Some
of the ministers of state there were who would
have accepted the resignation the Crown Prince
offered, and let him pass the throne to Nikolai,
his brother. But the Queen stepped in on their
counsels: "Gentlemen," she cried, "that must not
be, not for the country nor for Carol. It is Carol
who was born the ruler of Roumania."

To me, as we sat together there in her golden
room in the castle tower at Sinaia, the Queen inter-
polated: "I fought like a tiger for my son and
my country." Now hers is the point of view of
the royalist, to be sure. But it is absolutely sincere. You must hear it to the end.

This was her firstborn, you know, flesh of her
flesh. Think of the dreams she'd cherished for
him. It was straight from her heart she cried out
to her ministers: "Carol is of royal blood. A
marriage among the people is for him impossible. It is for a ruler to remain above the people,
a demigod. Carol was born the ruler of Roumania. And it's his duty to be."

"But," said some of the ministers, "he is bound
to a woman to whom he has given his word. Let
him keep his word and suffer banishment."

"No," vehemently insisted the Queen. "Gentlemen," she challenged, "who of you has not made
a mistake? And have you always paid for it?
Which of you is without fault in your relation to
some woman? Virtue is easy to preach to others."

She hesitated: "There is but one thing that

could stay my determination. There is but one thing I wish to know from you. Is this love between Zizi and Carol real love?" Some of the ministers thought it would not be eternal.

"Then," said the Queen, "I am free to interfere. The marriage shall be annulled."

It was. And Carol was sent on his journey around the world to forget. When he reached home again, he found visiting the Queen at the palace a young guest, the Princess Helene of Greece. She too had that magnetic influence and the charm of her youth. Carol, Crown Prince of Roumania, and Helene, Princess of Greece, were married in 1921. She is the sister of George of Greece, to whom Elizabeta was married a year later. Both seemed fortunate alliances. Carol's duty had been earnestly pointed out to him. He tried to take up the career for which he was royally intended. A little son, the baby Prince Mihai, was born within the year. The Queen had written, you remember, to old Nana of her great joy in her children.

Then it happened all over again. You can't say it was Zizi. Carol just couldn't keep his eyes on his career. Personal desire and another girl triumphed. It was the magnetic influence of a woman that drew him. And another. And another. Who shall say how many? Until now crown and kingdom and country have at last slipped quite completely from him. By act of Parliament and special ceremony of the Greek

Church, his little son, Mihai, has been declared in his stead the heir apparent for Roumania. And they have rung the bells again.

The bells! The bells! Those other bells, that rang in the joy of a kingdom. How they echo now in the heart of a woman! Bone of her bone, flesh of her flesh, you remember, she was creating a king.

Carol! Carol!

CHAPTER VIII

These Her People

YOU know how it has been said: "Uneasy lies the head that wears a crown." Well, hers doesn't. And perhaps it is because she has rested her head so much by keeping her crown in a glass case. Even as a Crown Princess she soon laid aside like that her coronet. She wound round her head instead the soft white *marama*. And she put on the tunic blouse and the short kilted *fota*. And attired like this in their own national dress, Marie of Roumania went out and sought and found her people.

They are a picturesque people. You have seen the Romany gypsy, who sometimes wanders into our western world with her bangled necklaces and her spangled costume that flames with yellow and red and orange as if she'd snatched it from an eastern sunset. As colorful as that are the Romany peasants on a saint's fête day, when they come streaming from their picturebook houses, the little cottages that Santa Claus might have hung on a Christmas tree. Then out from the church steps the priest, holding up the brilliant banners of a very decorative faith which illumines every public occasion. These are people for whom religion is still alight with wax tapers kept burning before pictured saints who stand in unbroken succession since St. Paul, the founder of this eastern earliest Christianity. And they are a primitive people. They are only forty-eight hours from Paris by the fast express that comes across the continent of Europe to make here its last stop. But they are more than a hundred years from New York when you see them doing their agriculture by hand. And they are a thousand years ago when you watch their wedding dance that commemorates the story of the Romans and the Sabine women. The bronze statue of Romulus and Remus standing in the Plaza Lispecani at Bucharest links them to that early empire many of whose most ancient customs and traditions still survive in their daily life. That is Roumania looking backward. There is also Roumania looking forward. It is led by a lady who can lay off a crown to lean down very close to the hearts of her people. So, listening softly, she has learned to know them and their needs. And so their humanity has come to hold for her a wider interest than all the royalty around her.

After all, she tells me, one can get just as tired of crown or coronet, even all set with diamonds, as one does of last year's hat. And the sameness of court circles grows much the same as the sameness of anywhere else. For over and over there are only the same pleasant things to be said: "How beauti-

ful are the grapes this year! How beautiful are
the flowers on the terrace! How beautiful is the
weather!" Or at any rate, "How beautiful it is
sure to be to-morrow!" Mashka, coming down the
grand staircase at Castle Pelasor, turned to me:
"Oh, for heaven's sake, if I could only think of
something new to say!" Outside the telegraph
wires of a continent were throbbing with history
white hot—some of it blood red—in the making.
But of all that, no echo was entering here, where
conversation was curtailed by the consideration
that every remark should contribute only to a
pleasant pæan of praise. Always in every royal
court it has been correct to create an atmosphere
of sugar and spice and everything nice to place before a Queen. It is a tribute that, as a survival of
ancient custom and ceremony, Her Majesty here in
Roumania still graciously accepts. But only as a
pretty painted picture. Now what is the real business of living?

And right down the steps of her throne this
Queen has gone trippingly to find out. Let no
bowing courtier attempt to tell Marie of Roumania the moon is made of green cheese. She's
sure to start off for a look herself. "There is
nothing my mother may not wish to do," Nicky
says. "And the more unusual it is, the more she
will wish to do it." In support of this contention
Nicky refers in particular to a visit to an ancient
convent isolated on a mountain peak in Greece.
On arrival there, it was learned by the royal party

that the only means of entrance was by a basket in which a visitor, perilously suspended in mid-air, must be drawn up the wall of rock some hundreds of feet high. Indeed! But that was an adventure not to be missed. A Queen stepped lightly into the basket, comfortably curled herself up, and gave the signal that hoisted her aloft.

"Well," laughs the Queen as Nicky finishes his story, "I'm sure if I'd been in Paradise like Eve, I too should have tasted the apple. And anyhow, I know Greece a lot better than Sophie my cousin, once Queen there, ever did. Sophie," concludes Marie, "just can't stand fleas."

But the Queen of Roumania never has hesitated before reality. She never has shrunk back from experience. And she knows her Roumania. It was as a young Crown Princess that she first rode away from a court that bored her to gallop on her horse alone over mountain and plain. So she went out to see the land that history had been holding for her coming. Since then she has ridden far, oh! so far, that she has indeed made this country her country. It is a country crumbling and battle scarred, the rehabilitation of which began as it were but yesterday. Much of what might have been the accumulated treasure and inheritance of the centuries is gone. Terrible and wanton was the destruction wrought by enemy hordes who in wave after wave of invasion swept over this territory. Very many of the ancient landmarks like the lovely castles and the stately cathedrals so carefully preserved in more fortunate lands were here ruthlessly destroyed. Others just wearily decayed through the centuries, finally falling to pieces for lack of funds to keep them in repair. It was, you see, not only that at the time of the withdrawal of the Roman legions who had made this land *Romania* there was left no protection against the neighboring barbarians. But when it finally fell under the suzerainty of the Sublime Porte, the Turks imposed such devastating taxes as drained the land of all resources. King Carol in his work of restoration had labored indefatigably and effectually for fundamentals. And his foundations were well builded. But the girl who was to give Roumania its high place among the nations found on her arrival here no splendid art galleries hung with historic canvasses of old families; no palaces so ancestral that they might echo with a long royal line; no state treasury holding a priceless collection of jewels and trophies of war. She did find, however, a country with a very old-world charm that everywhere invites you. In response to that call, one rides out over roads the Emperor Trajan built, into vast horizons that roll wide southeast to the Danube River and lift high northwest in the gray peaks of the Transylvania Alps. There are deep forests dark green with old mysteries. There are wide wind-blown plains silent with an ancient stillness. Above both stretches the sky space where hang in gorgeous pictures the far-flung Roumanian sunrise and sunset. Then, high above the rest of the landscape, towering into the very clouds, stand the mighty feudal fortresses that have defied attack and time.

These, like the ancient medieval Bran which the Queen has converted into her lovely romantic castle, are situated on the very top of the most inaccessible mountain peaks, the walls themselves in irregular shape following the edges of the summit, so that every precipice and chasm yawning beneath contributed to the impregnability of the primitive stronghold. Through a country like this, all reminiscent of knights of old who engaged in tournament and adventure, the long Roumanian roads wind on and on. Along this very way went crusaders bound for Jerusalem. Constantinople afforded the opportunity for a break in their long journey. But finally as travel increased, with more crusaders and more merchants always coming, another nearer stopping place catered to their comfort. Where the farm of the peasant Bucur and a few others clustered along the Dumbovitza, the little river that is tributary to the Danube, rose a Han. The Han was a "guesthouse" which made crude provision for travelers, who must bring their own food and bedding but found here a roof for shelter and an enclosure with locked gates for safety at night. Finally, along about the time that Columbus discovered America, began here Bucharest, which by the year 1700 had grown into a populous city of 50,000 inhabitants. And everybody came to Bucharest along the long Roumanian roads.

Very little have they changed since then, except that the knights in armor have passed on never to return. Still the same ancient crosses of gray granite before which they did their devotions serve as the worn and weatherbeaten wayside shrines of prayer for every passing peasant. Still travelers pause for refreshment at wells with bucket and curb and well sweep like those in Palestine. Still tends her geese by the roadside the woman with distaff and spindle, dexterously twirling and twisting and spinning the wool from which she will weave on a hand loom all the cloth for her household purposes, even as did those diligent women commended in Bible times. Still in the fields white-smocked peasants, dressed as their Roman forebears, are cutting rye with scythes swung in shining rhythmic strokes, while after them even as Ruth followed Boaz come the women with sickles who will bind the grain in sheaves. Later, with a flail consisting of two hard sticks held together by a leather thong, it is threshed out to make black bread. Still along the roads are always coming the slow-moving carts of the peasants taking produce to market, the crude hand-made, home-made carts drawn by teams of great yoked oxen with spreading horns. And at sunset come the herds of goats or the flocks of sheep with their tinkling bells and the soft whistling of the shepherds calling each to his own.

Few are the houses along the roads, because in those long centuries under Turkish dominion, there was demanded each year a certain toll of young girls for the Sultan's harem and of young boys for the army; and these could be snatched up anywhere along a public road. The people therefore cautiously placed their houses far back and hidden. Or you find them in clustering groups through which the road runs as the single village street. Such quaint little cottages from which Miss Muffet or Little Red Riding Hood or even Mother Goose herself might be expected any minute to step forth. I think I like best those with the heavy shaggy thatched roofs hugging them close and hanging so low that you may touch the eaves by lifting your hand. The red roofs of slate and corrugated tile make lovely splotches of color against a background of blue sky. And the shingle roofs are most curiously done with here and there a lifted place like a raised eyelid above an opening not large enough to be a window but known as "the eye of the house." The houses are of home made brick overlaid with plaster, which is usually whitewashed fresh at Easter time each year. Only the "wash" doesn't have to be white. Just as well, it may be lavender or blue or red or Pompeian pink. I know one entire village all done in lavender with coral red roofs. Now and again you come to a white house all painted over the front with garlands of flowers, which means that the family here has a girl in bloom, a daughter who's ready for marriage.

To these color effects now add the "trimmings," scroll-sawed fretwork in wood, nut brown stain. In arabesque pattern and flower pattern and all sorts of fanciful design, it runs along the gabled edges of the roofs and around little porches and tiny balconies. So that these seem little embroidered houses. There are always casement windows that stand ajar, with pots of red geraniums or brimming boxes of flowers set on the sill. And always in front of each little house there is a yard spilling over with gay flowers. Purple hyacinths and yellow daffodils here, the Queen tells me, are up earlier in the spring; orange marigolds and red dahlias last later in the fall than anywhere else. Flowers are so happy with these people who fairly love them into growth. A peasant's passion for color spends itself in three ways: in the decoration of his costume with embroideries; in the laying out of gardens, even of vegetable gardens that he makes veritable tapestries down in the earth; and in hand-made rugs woven in a riot of pattern and color caught from nature around him.

It was into a landscape like this that the young Crown Princess rode in the autumn, when the little houses are all festooned with ropes of red and green peppers and clusters of yellow ears of corn; in the winter, when they are blanketed soft and silent and white and glistening with deep snow; in the spring, when they are set against a fairy background of fruit trees in bloom; in the summer, when they are all a burning glow of fiery flowers. This was her first enchantment. But soon it was more than the beauty of the landscape with its witching charm that enthralled her. She wanted to see beyond the casement windows and the open doorways. And so at last she found herself looking straight into the souls of the common people.

It is a contact that she never has lost. Many a time when another Queen might be sitting idly on a throne holding a scepter, you may find Marie of Roumania sitting on a low stool in some peasant's cottage learning all about the business of living. When she comes formally to her villages, as you have seen, they ring the church bells and hang out all the bright banners of their beautiful rugs·in greeting. And the people kiss her hand, sometimes the hem of her skirt and even her feet, touching their foreheads to the ground in obeisance. At first, as she tells me, she did not know what to make of such homage. But as she became herself more eastern, she was able to accept it graciously in the spirit of reverent adoration in which it was offered. Now no one of the villagers themselves enters more thoroughly than she into the festal spirit of these occasions, made impressive with ancient manners and tradition. But the Queen likes also to come at times unheralded. As Marie of Roumania, with no ceremony to separate her, she may then gather her people close. Then it is, sitting on a low stool, she takes their black-eyed babies in her arms. And who knows better how to hold a baby to her bosom, to cuddle a small head in that divine hollow God made in her arm! And with a sympathy that can o'erleap all caste, she clasps the hand of a woman in sorrow. She touches gently the bowed head of some unkempt hairy old man. She smiles into the happy eyes of young lovers. She counts a soldier's medals.

It's marvelous how she never mixes their joys or their troubles. She knows the aches and pains and heart throbs of each village from every other. She remembers unerringly which girl it is who's next to be married, that this old woman has rheumatism in the knees, and at that house lives the man who is going blind. Especially always she remembers just how many children a woman has borne and how many buried. All these things, however, she lets them tell her over and over. And always she listens well, with that quiet patience which so eases aching hearts.

From their lips as she sat side by side with them like this, she has told me, she first learned the Roumanian language. Word by word and phrase by phrase, she picked it up. There is a trace of the Slavic, Bulgarian, and Turkish contacts through which it has come; but it is a speech that has remained nevertheless largely Latin like its original source. To that western half of the Roman Empire concentrated at Byzantium, which the Emperor Constantine made his capital city, may be traced also most of this people's traditions and customs. That these are sometimes Greek in character is because Constantinople adopted the Greek culture. That they are sometimes Turkish is because when that city fell to the Saracens the Turkish overlordship still kept the Roumanians close in touch with Constantinople. Much nearer through the ages they lived to the Orient of their close affiliation than to the Occident of their geographical location. The bright embroideries of their holiday costumes repeat sometimes classic Greek and Roman patterns and sometimes shimmer with Turkish spangles. For the Queen's coming, they open their marriage chests and show her their "dozen dozen" of everything. This store of linen, all spun and woven and embroidered by hand, is made ready by a girl for her wedding day, to supply the needs of a new household for at least a generation. They bring also their *Salbas* for the Queen to count. This is the dot with which a bride goes to her husband. It consists of gold coins suspended from a black velvet ribbon worn as a necklace about the throat and as bracelets on the wrists. And every woman wishes to show the colorful embroidered costume that is her wedding gown; this, reserved for holiday occasions, is expected to last a lifetime. And in it, the wearer will also be buried on that other great occasion, the funeral, which vies with the wedding in importance; always it is looked forward to with as careful planning, that one may arrive at the gates of heaven looking her very best for St. Peter to see.

It is, of course, the rich peasant household that can afford such splendid equipment of embroideries. Many there are for whom hard toil leaves little time for elaborate decoration of life. Living arrangements in a two room cottage, it is true, are simplified to a minimum. And also magnified to a maximum. There is no complicated cooking, because there is nothing complicated to cook for peasant fare. Mamiliga, their cornmeal mush, with a slice of onion or red pepper and a piece of goat's cheese constitutes a dinner. But there is all the wool and the cloth, the rugs and the clothing for the women of the family to make, while the men make the shoes and the furniture and the farm implements. Then both together work always side by side in the fields. Apparently the women have never thought to protest the custom. Certain it is that they expect and accept it. Perhaps even they prefer to play a part in nature's great drama of seed time and harvest. These are, you see, uneventful lives except for the mysteries they meet in birth and death, and the two pageants prepared for them in royalty and religion. Both of the latter they like splendid with pomp and ceremony and colorful with custom. Of this the Queen of Roumania takes cognizance. Though no one can more easily and more lightly lay aside the trappings of royalty, she keeps them carefully at hand for dress parade. Not only her people require that a ruler shall be ready to be regal, but she herself regards it as a duty.

Only after you have stepped off from the western world into the middle ages here, will you really understand that point of view. All that the peasant may never hope to attain, he may still have joy in looking at. Serfdom, you see, is recent here. A sovereign is yet very near to God. And one's "betters" not far below. Feudalism has so lately faded from the picture, that it is not forgot. Many of its fixings you find still retained in the accustomed gestures of everyday life. This is the land of *sarut mana,* "I kiss the hand." The custom is not confined to court circles. It is as commonly done as in America a man lifts his hat. You may not enter a drawing-room without its occurrence. Even in a newspaper office in Bucharest, when I made a professional call, the editor kissed my hand. And it is not only the courtesy that a man offers a woman. It is also a reverence expected from the peasants by the upper classes. Every passing contact is recognized by the regular formula; a servant entering the room to make your bed, repeats in the accustomed apologetic murmur, "Sarut mana."

There are other quaint customs surviving in this very old world to make everyday affairs seem set for a play on the stage. The national holiday on May 10, marking Roumania's independence from Turkey and corresponding in sentiment to

our own American Fourth of July, is kept of
course with all national rejoicing. But there are
besides some thirty-two saints' days each year
which serve as occasion for making happy holiday. Toil may be hard between. But, you see,
more often even than once in two weeks, the
church and the calendar offer a red letter day,
when every one dons his beautiful best clothes
and the men put peacock feathers in their hats.
Religious rites are soon over. The gypsy
musician for the village gets out his *cobsa,* and
there begins the dance of the Hora which is the
real national amusement. In a wide, wide circle
that includes everybody hand in hand, the people
fling themselves into the rhythmic movement with
an abandon that is joyous and complete. Then
there is the longer festival of the Rusali in
August. This is a survival of the nature worship
of the Greeks. The Rusali are three genii, who
by three days of ceremonial observance may be
placated so they will not harm the crops. Other
evil spirits are warded off when the village priest
in satin vestments comes once a month to bless the
house. From a basin of holy water held by an
acolyte he has sprinkled the doorway by means
of a small whisk broom tied with a red ribbon.
There, not the devil himself will dare to enter
here!

Besides, as the Lares and Penates protected the
ancient Roman household, so the ikon guards the
Roumanian family of to-day. In every house, set

in a niche in the wall or on a bracket in the corner, you will find this replica of the chosen patron saint, before which a lighted taper is kept ever burning. This, the ikon, is a religious emblem belonging distinctively to eastern Christianity. The early Greek Church fathers had read in their Bible the command against the graven image. Still, the people wanted something to see. So the ikon is a compromise between an image and a picture. The face of the saint painted on the background of wood, as also the hands and the feet, are shown through cutouts in the overlaid metal of gold or silver known as the *viza,* which itself is modeled in relief to represent the folds of the saint's clothing.

While ikon and ceremony are trusted to keep the household safe from harm, there may be emergencies that require other appeal. Are the crops, for instance, threatened with drought? There is help for that. The mayor issues a call. And the villagers led by the priests, carrying sacred relics brought from the church, march about the fields to the chant of a Te Deum; then all kneel in prayer for rain. Or if the drought is widespread and threatens to become the country's calamity, there is one powerful to make direct intervention above. St. Dmitrie, 500 years dead, in the Metropole on the hill in Bucharest, is a national possession. He will intercede. In the massive, wonderfully wrought silver coffin, St. Dmitrie is borne aloft in solemn procession through the streets of the city, while the people pray. Only three years ago, there came a definite answer. Scarcely had the splendidly robed procession returned with its sacred burden to the Metropole, when there occurred a downpour of rain that drenched a parched and thirsty land and made plenty in place of famine.

Nor is it in Roumania only that the power of St. Dmitrie is recognized. The relic came, I believe, originally from Russia. And the Bulgarians so desired to have it that at the time of the occupation of Bucharest by the Central Powers during the war, they attempted to seize it. But they were foiled. *"Sfint* Dmitrie," the Roumanians triumphantly tell you, "made himself heavy." So that all the soldiers who marched on the Metropole were unable to lift from the floor the massive silver coffin. It is a habit that *Sfint* Dmitrie has when he does not wish to be disturbed. Even sometimes when the Roumanians have wished to ask for rain, the saint has "made himself heavy" and refused. Could the coffin on these occasions have been nailed to the floor? That's an infidel idea which no true believer would entertain.

This which is called the Greek Orthodox Church is still as orthodox as when it started. It is alike the church of Roumania, Russia, Serbia, Bulgaria and Greece. Not from the latter country does it take its name, but from the Hellenic culture prevailing at the court where Christianity

under the patronage of an emperor first became
flourishing and fashionable. When Paul had
established the church at Constantinople, he sent
out others of the disciples to carry the cross northward. It may have been Andrew who brought
the faith to this Roumania. Meanwhile Peter
had set up at Rome the western church. Differences developing between the two foremost
apostles you find reflected in the separate ritual
and dogma of the Greek and the Roman churches
of to-day. Even their architecture is different.
After you have come over the Carpathians, you
see instead of the church spire and the Gothic
form, the Byzantine church with gilded domes
surmounted by the Greek cross. But of the prior-
ity of this eastern Christianity there can be no
question. Twenty-five years before the Bible was
translated into English, they had here the New
Testament in Roumanian.

They are still fundamental about it. And religion is a chief aspect of the country. The church
structures that have survived date back usually not
farther than the 16th and 17th centuries. But it is
these that constitute really the national exhibit, to
be shown as elsewhere in Europe they show you old
palaces. And I know of no other land where religion has so richly beautiful a setting. It is not
only that the Metropole in Bucharest is magnificent. But every little country church is also a gem
of Byzantine coloring in miniature. However remote and obscure these little churches may be, you

will find there richly painted ikons, lovely embroideries, beautifully illuminated old Bibles. These are cherished as a kingdom's treasure. For this reason, the churches in ancient times were often fortified. You see them now surrounded by a high stone wall, against which all the way around the inside are built the cell-like, little one-room houses occupied by the monks. The entrance is through a gateway surmounted by a bell tower, the whole structure with the church in the center having been arranged as a fortified stronghold. The church is square or oblong, often with an entrance like the porch of Solomon's Temple at Jerusalem. The doors admitting to the vestibule may be of bronze or of carved wood; so marvelous in execution are some of these that they are now being removed to the museum in Bucharest for safekeeping.

Sometimes even the outside walls of these ancient little churches are frescoed with a frieze of saints. Inside, always the walls are painted with pictures. These are saints and heroes of Biblical story, and along with them in his crown and ermine robes the patron Prince who built the church, with his wife and family beside him. At Sinaia in the latest church, left by King Carol as his memorial, you find him pictured on the wall along with Elizabeth his Queen and the little daughter who was their only child. On the walls of the adjacent church dating back to 1638 appear the Prince and Princess Cantacuzene and their some sixteen children. Curiously round-eyed, rigid of line and stiff in posture, these archaic frescoed folk stare out from their setting in the centuries. But all have been touched with the patina of time that has turned to the loveliest coloring their red and blue robes and golden haloes. Then for the most beautiful exhibit of all, see the ikonistas.

This, the altar screen, literally a "picture stand," presents in the Greek church the opportunity for rich ornamentation with which no feature of a western church may compare. The altar screen is the partition some ten or twelve feet high, which shuts off from the rest of the edifice the holy of holies known as the "Sanctuary," on the altar of which reposes always the sacred, wondrously wrought, silver bound copy of the Gospels. The screen consists of pictures of the Apostles and the Holy Family, each picture set in its separate gold frame and all joined together to form one complete wall of gold and color, the ikonista. An inner rotunda nearest the ikonista has some six or eight high-backed seats ranged against the wall and reserved for royalty or nobility. The outer auditorium beyond is for the people. And there are no pews. Even at the greatest church of all, the Metropole of Bucharest, the people throughout the entire service, when not kneeling, are standing. Because at church, you see, they are in the presence of God.

They would not presume to sit in the presence of the ruler of the universe. Religion here is real. O, how these people believe in God! See the Rou-

manian peasant in prayer at the Metropole. Note
the beauty of devotion as at length it comes to shine
in his illumined face. He has dropped on his knees
on the floor. His eyes are closed, his folded hands
uplifted. His lips move silently and he crosses
himself. Now he postures until even his forehead
touches the cold stone floor in his deep abasement.
Over and over like this, he does his adoration. And
at last it has occurred: see his face transfigured
with the rapt look that reveals his soul's attain-
ment of complete communion with the infinite.

All around rises the fragrant odor of incense:
black-bearded priests in long black gowns are
swinging jeweled censors as they pass to and fro
among the people. The soft light from stained
glass windows enfolds the worshippers: on one side
of the room are the men in embroidered sheepskin
coats and on the other side women in embroidered
petticoats and with white-veiled or red-kerchiefed
headdress. And side by side with these are others
in plain store clothes. There are too some of the
upper classes, men in black frock suits and women
in costumes from Paris. Each worshipper on
entering has lighted a wax taper. Now these
countless tapers, set before the holy pictures, burn
like so many flickering little golden stars of light.
Wondrously wrought lamps of silver and gold set
with precious stones hang from the ceiling, re-
lieving the darkness of the high spaces. Through
the rich gloom the ikonistas flash colorful and
golden. Before its Holy Doors as they open and

close during the intervals of the service stands the
Metropolitan in jeweled mitre and stiff vestments
of old brocade shimmering with gold and silver
thread. And see, crowding every space of wall and
pilaster and dome, the vast pictured company of
gold-haloed saints. As you glance upward into
the deep well of the great dome, it seems literally
as if heaven had opened and all its company were
looking down on the congregation. Before this
throng of witnesses, generation after generation of
men has unrolled the record of its soul, and the
heartbreak and grief of the ages have gone up to
God in prayer.

Now listen to a church service unchanged for
more than a thousand years. It is rhythmically
intoned and musically chanted. There is no me-
chanical instrument. But the human voice alone
gives sublime expression to the soul in music surpassing in majestic beauty that of any other faith.
All the gamut of human emotions is run in measured cadences as the voices sink low in the despair
of sin and sorrow and grief, only later to rise by
stages in high aspiration to the exaltation of tran-
scendent joy. Then hear the choir in ringing
triumph proclaim, "Holy, Holy, Holy, Lord of
Sabbaoth, heaven and earth are full of Thy glory!"
The service closes. The worshippers file rever-
ently in line before the altar to salute the wonder-
working ikons with a holy kiss. And on the faces
of all the common people as they pass out into the
porch there is still reflected the glory of religion.

You see how Roumania with its embroidered peasants and its Byzantine churches is like a colorful mosaic from some far yesterday. Somehow the ages seem to have missed it as they went on their way making over the rest of the earth. Roumania is as old as that. But I would have you know that Roumania is new too. I know of nowhere else in the world where medievalism so meets modernism coming right down Main street. The city of Bucharest is laid out irregularly in curving circles where the ancient Boyars, first coming to town, erected their city residences with all of their household retainers encamped about them. But one street that goes straight through the city from the race course to the river, is the Calea Victorei, the Avenue of Victory as they named it after the troops came down it from Plevna. It is the Fifth Avenue of Bucharest, on which is situated the National Theater, the Post Office, the smart shops, the Cercle Militaire, the university that King Carol founded, the most pretentious residences and the Palatul Victorei, The Royal Victory Palace itself. And Bucharest, which Baedecker before the war listed with a population of some 300,000, is now a city of nearly a million.

Yet still down this fashionable Calea Victorei comes on occasion the splendid *Sfint* Dmitrie procession. And almost any day you may meet another with a band playing softly, wondrously, as only a Roumanian band may play, a slow measured dirge; men in silver-braided black coats and

cocked hats, bearing aloft on long black poles high
lighted lanterns; priests in robes of vivid color and
tall purple hats; in front of the procession, two carrying between them on a great silver platter the
coliva which is really the funeral cake of Virgil;
and in the hearse drawn by four horses hooded to
their eyes and covered to their heels with a black
velvet panoply, the passenger who rides to the
grave carries always in his quiet folded hand a
coin. It is the coin once required by Charon for
ferry fare across the Styx, but now by adaptation
intended for St. Peter at the gates of heaven. So
in a land picturesque with ceremony, ancient custom survives. Still down this same Main Street
to-day too, the slow moving ox-cart takes its even
way, with a white-smocked peasant in a black
sheepskin hat, holding the reins over the backs of
his great yoked animals. And the low swinging
carriage, the *birja,* remains a customary public
conveyance, with a driver, the *birjar,* clad always
in a blue velvet mantle falling full skirted to his
ankles and encircled at his ample waist line with a
silken sash in red or pink or maybe sky blue. Now
there have also arrived as many motor cars as in
any other twentieth century city. And Bucharest
has the most convenient line of motor busses,
operated by a man from New York, that I have
seen anywhere in the world. But note that at these
strange interloping vehicles the white oxen with
their wide-spreading horns stare solemnly. And
the *birjar* behind his lean little horse looks con-

temptuously. Both, you see, have been here so long before. Between them let the automobiles with their clanging klaxons, dodge as best they may. "Hopi," calls a blue-vested *birjar:* and all entanglement of traffic makes way at his command. But sometimes down the street comes a polished mahogany Rolls-Royce car; to this both the white-smocked peasant and the blue-velveted *birjar,* bending low with uncovered heads, do a beautiful profound obeisance. And all the lean little horses and the great white-yoked oxen stop in their tracks, while a lovely Lady wearing about her head the white *marama,* passes by with a smile and a wave of her hand. The Rolls-Royce turns in at the Palatul Victorei. Modernism is leading medievalism happily right at her chariot wheels.

It has been all at the wave of a woman's hand. Scarcely ever has the Queen's scepter moved at all. But from out a very old-world background, even right above the uneven cobblestone pavements the centuries have trod, is emerging to-day a changing city. Already the apartment house begins to elbow the old Roumanian residence of Arabesque architecture. Among the two and three story buildings are rising those of six and seven, a new city hall, an imposing railroad station, a large and beautiful University building to replace the earlier smaller one. Western culture is coming. In moving pictures right here on the Calea Victorei Jesse Lasky's "Covered Wagon" has brought the Browns, the Kents, and the Woodfields for these

eastern folk to know. American typewriters,
American plows, American shoes, American Fords
are announced in the store windows. The Hotel
Athenee Palace has American bath tubs and
American heat.

And see, across its front an illuminated sign that
proclaims the last word in up-to-date equipment,
"Bar American." Well, at Bar American have
been put across some of the great business deals of
the world. Ali the Arab in red Turkish fez dis-
penses with equal equanimity a whisky and soda
for the Englishman from Threadneedle Street or a
Manhattan cocktail for the American from Wall
Street. These captains of finance on the trail of
oil are registered at the desk in Roumanian. They
are welcomed with eastern hospitality by a hotel
manager who speaks French, the polite language
here of the upper classes. Mirzah the tall Turk,
smiling first with his hand on his heart, has then
bent low to receive on his back their luggage. The
elevator man who has brought them up in the
"lift" has called out the floor in German. A maid
may make their beds in Hungarian. A boy very
likely blacks their shoes in Russian. When they
must know what all of these are talking about, it is
Constantine, the porter at the front entrance, who
can tell. He says it too in perfectly good American that came from Youngstown, Ohio. Once he
worked there in the steel mills, before he was
caught up in the whirlwind of war to be flung back
here on his native soil.

Roumania has, as you may discover, a diverse population to-day. Some of its numerous minorities are of recent acquisition. When the Queen of Roumania had finished with that peace conference at Paris, she came back leading long-lost provinces overlaid with other languages than their mother tongue. And her capital city begins now to reflect the prosperity flowing to it from a kingdom increased by an area rich in oil and minerals. But variegated as it may be with recent additions of territory, this land remains distinctively early Roman in character. And eighty per cent of its population is to be found among the peasants.

Mingled among them are the gypsies, the *tzigani,* as they are called, who add their own note to make this a Roumania so brightly colorful. Where the gypsies of mysterious charm really came from I suppose no one on earth knows. They arrived here with the Romans. But they came even then from a much longer ago. It has been surmised by some that once in ancient Egypt they served the cult of Isis. And that at least might account for the gift of divination which they have from some far past. For scoff as you will, the fact remains that every little while a Romany gypsy's fortune-telling comes startlingly true. The peasants of Roumania bring to them their dreams and accept the interpretation thereof like modern Freudians. When the peasants here were serfs, the gypsies were slaves, not set free until some time even later. The peasants did the work in the fields and the gypsies were the household servants for the great Boyars. Sometimes still they are butlers and cooks. Some are soldiers in the army. Some live as traveling tinkers mending pots and pans. Most naturally of all, they take to the out-of-doors.

Now before the Hotel Athenee Palace, hear a musical voice repeating "Mimosa fromosa, Mimosa fromosa." It is Annunciata, the Romany gypsy, calling her wares. In her wistful dark beauty, she dances on the sidewalk and sells flowers. Her arms are full of the spraying yellow blooms. Annunciata has eyes whose black-fringed depths reflect the dreams of all the ages; and beautiful, regular little teeth that flash so white without benefit of anybody's modern dentifrice. Her hips are slender. And the ankles above her small bare brown feet are shapely as any lady's. Over her shining black hair is tied a red handkerchief. She wears swinging earrings of coral and a red coral necklace about her brown throat. "Mimosa fromosa, Mimosa fromosa." It is Annunciata selling flowers. And so wistfully pretty she is. Her of all others none who has been to Bucharest may ever forget.

As street vendors, the gypsies are everywhere familiar figures along the city sidewalks. The men carry shallow baskets or trays, hung one from each end of a bent pole slung across the shoulders; and on these trays are spread for sale the fruits of the season, in the summer, red strawberries or in the fall, purple plums and golden grapes arranged with white walnut meats on green leaves. Both men and women work together wherever there are building operations; all of the plaster work is done by gypsies. But these you meet along the pavements of Bucharest are not resplendently appareled like those sophisticated exhibits of their race who come wandering over the world. The men wear, like other laborers in Bucharest, the tight white woolen trousers and the long white linen smocks held at the waist with a red belt. But these garments on a gypsy are always in rags and tatters and he seldom or never has on his feet the *opinciu,* the home-made leather sandals. The women are most often attired in cast-off clothing of the gentry. Annunciata dances on the sidewalk in a faded purple skirt, full gathered, that must have come down from sometime in the nineties. You see they are squalidly poor and so recently up from slavery, these children of nature. At work on a building, they comfortably stretch on its floors to spend the night. There were gypsies I saw making repairs on the Theneum, Bucharest's beautiful concert hall. Under the nearest electric light in a public square had been assembled a pile of lumber, carefully piled there and high. And in the leisure hours of evening after their hod-carrying was done, two gypsy women perched easily on its summit as serenely as under any historic lamplight of a happy home. Only they weren't darning stockings, of which they have none to trouble them. But with the innate eternal feminine love of finery, there they sat high up in the night above a city pavement, calmly embroidering their blouses.

Literally carefree as the birds these gypsies live, you see. And just as naturally they make music too. Every little village has its own *lautari,* the gypsy who on flute or lute plays for all marriages, funerals, and fête-day dancing. In the orchestra of every café in Bucharest, it is gypsies who make that music, witching with a melody that sets the pulses throbbing, haunting with a sweetness long drawn out that melts the heart to tears. Who once has heard a violin for which gypsy fingers draw the bow is tuned for strains celestial. From the musical centers of Europe, they send down here for a tryout their new stars in the making. It was to the Atheneum Caruso came for his début. Passing this critical concert hall audience, one is certain to find himself on the pleasant road to fame. They know music in Roumania. They have learned it at its source, straight from the gypsy's soul.

Highly educated, sophisticated, polished with a Paris contact, are the upper classes of Roumania. With their great estates in the country and their city houses at Yassy or at Bucharest, they usually spend also some months each year in that city of France which is the world's capital of culture. There are twenty which are called the "real first families," who are direct descendants of the early ruling Princes. Some two hundred more have come from the old Boyar nobility. Added to these are about one thousand other families who are also included among Roumania's aristocracy.

Now it was to the common people that the Queen of Roumania from the first was deeply drawn. About herself you feel that there is something fine and primeval. See in her red slippers and her swinging embroidered skirt, how she steps off with the dignity and the freedom of a peasant. Like them she loves the sweet smell of the ground after rain, and all of the wide out-of-doors. She knows intimately the forests and the plains and the grain fields and the long dusty roads. And every picturesque custom and tradition she has absorbed and come to understand. It was to the cottages she turned at first. But neither has she missed the castle halls. Through old Moldavia and the Bucovina when we went in that Tren Regale we stopped at some of the great estates. I saw her admire in their drawing-rooms their rugs and their tapestries and the ancestral painted portraits of the turbaned Boyars on their walls. She sat on their stone terraces, framed with formal flower beds and clipped yew trees, with the cool silvery sound of falling water in the fountains around making pleasant summer melody. And she drank their Turkish coffee and their Roumanian liqueurs. She walked through their vineyards up and down all the long lines of the vines, tasting every variety of grape, the red ones and the blue and the purple and the golden-green ones. She lingered in their gardens, those marvelous gardens unrolled in carpets of color that seemed to stretch in acres of landscape bloom.

And she held their children too in her arms. We came to a christening. It was in that Bucovina so lately acquired from Austria, where the population, though 60 per cent Roumanian, is still 40 per cent Slav. The baby had been born to an Austrian Count of Italian origin and his wife, a Russian Princess who had fled from the Bolsheviks. Both are now, through the change in political circumstance, Roumanian subjects. And the Queen had come to stand godmother to their child. Garlands of evergreens and bright Roumanian flags made a festive background. There was first a great banquet with rare viands served on china that bore two ancient crests. Then in the drawing room, titled relatives crowding about the Queen with the baby in her arms, came the Roman Catholic baptismal rite. Tiny little fingers had clasped tightly and happily the priceless string of pearls and emeralds that hung from Her Majesty's throat. The priest in his vestments stepped forward. At the first contact with the holy water he sprinkled, there arose an angry scream of protest. But the Queen gathered the white embroidered bundle close, to murmur soft comfort: "There, there, is it then so terrible a thing to be made a Christian!"

And I noticed how deftly she held to her bosom Marie Dorothea Isabella Elizabetha Eugenia, daughter of Count D—— S—— R—— who once had been an alien enemy. Now that was characteristic of the Queen. "How can the baby help the war?" she declared as we drove away.

Earlier in the day some of her entourage who had learned of her intention had whispered in protest: "But Your Majesty, the family is more German than it should be."

"Well," promptly responded the Queen, "if that is so, all the more reason why the baby should be baptized as Roumanian as it can be."

Later, to the royal court at Sinaia she announced: "Since we are now all here together, I have something to say. As you all very well know, when I am planning to do anything that may cause a row, I do it first and talk about it afterward. Well, yesterday I was godmother at a christening." Then she went on detailing all about the alien ancestry and the whispered protest. "Anyhow," she concluded, "I've sponsored that child as a Christian and now it's done. As my godchild, I venture she'll grow up a true patriot. And her family I now feel is as Roumanian as any of the oldest Moldavian line. I know what I am doing."

Ah, so much that another sovereign might never know nor ever understand, this Queen of Roumania has come to know. Royalist that she was born, she must of course remain. "I do not believe in equality," she says. "God makes one class higher than another. Some of us have been born to high place. Mine happens to be the highest of all. But God put me here. And if I were to resign my job to-morrow, who could do it better? Cer-

tainly not my maid. And it would be even unkind
to impose on her tasks to which she is not equal
and for which she is totally unprepared. How, for
instance, would she like being obliged to receive
a Metropolitan or a diplomat? Why, she'd be
even more uncomfortable than I should be sewing
on my own buttons. For both of us, it would be
utter folly that we should turn about in any such
fashion.

"On the other hand it does humiliate me to need
so much service that I require twenty-three people
standing round to wait on me. But there are somehow so many things to be done and I haven't myself
hands enough to do them all. Now I do not believe in equality but there is such a thing as justice.
It is not fair for one class to have all the hard times
in life and another class more than its share of comfort. So what can we who are higher up do to
make life easier for the others? That is the question with which we are now confronted. By way
of compensation, if I am a person requiring so
much service, then I must find some way to give
in return for what I receive. I must give, too, that
which people want. My people are a peasant
people. What they want, I have discovered, is
land . . ."

Oh, Roumania is as you have seen, as old as its
origin. But it is new too, as new as its future.
Have you heard of the agrarian legislation that is
rushing evolution here where otherwise revolution
might be running red? Why, a land like this may

be even o'erleaping to-day to catch up with to-morrow.

Uneasy lies the head that wears a crown! Hers doesn't. Baptizing their babies, walking their vineyards, visiting their churches, revering their ikons, sitting in cottages, and soothing sorrows! And partitioning the land! These people she has made her people.

CHAPTER IX

Maria Regina

THE King is dead! Long live the King! Up at Sinaia at the castle in the forest, Carol I. of Roumania lay white and cold and still, with lighted waxen candles about him casting flickering shadows through a darkened room. Down in Bucharest, Ferdinand I. of Roumania amid the breathless hush of a crowded House of Parliament, had taken the sovereign's oath, by the help of God, to lead and serve this people so long as his life should last. Outside now in the streets the populace, massed in a dense throng, had broken out in the cheering that acclaimed him King.

Then hark! There was more. A new refrain had started. With ever increasing volume it rose to a mighty chorus: "Maria Regina! Maria Regina!" The people wanted Her.

In response to their call, she stepped out onto a balcony above them. And she had arrived at the hour of triumph in her career. It was in the thirty-eighth year of her age. "Maria Regina! Maria Regina! Maria Regina!"

In wave after wave of that sound that was like music in her ears, their adoration and their adula-

215

tion enwrapped and enfolded her. And how mingled were her emotions! She had but just come from a solemn requiem mass at the Metropole. She had kissed dead lips. Tears filled her eyes. There was the sense of the swift rush of events that had crowded her onward here. But who was she to hold back God's appointed plan? Her cue had been called on the stage prepared for her. So she moved to the new moment that now claimed her. The inevitable grief of life gave way to the inevitable joy of life. She breathed in ecstasy. Then she smiled in radiance upon her Roumania.

Higher and higher rose the cry of greeting that swept upward to her from an entire city: "Maria Regina! Maria Regina!" There was no mistaking the tribute. It was indeed the heart of a nation that was voiced in the swelling cadence of feeling and emotion ringing out in that mighty rhythm: "Maria Regina! Maria Regina!" So they were still calling as she stepped from sight.

Her supreme exaltation was finished. There would be occasions more outwardly colorful and splendid. There would be glittering pageants to do honor to the power and charm of her personality. But never again could she experience that first-time exquisite thrill in response to the devotion of a people naming her Queen because they loved her so. And now a tie had been forged, a trust imposed that would be forever. The transfiguration of service for which she was destined was about to begin. Already the Roumanian sky was overcast by the dark shadows of the war clouds enveloping Europe. It had been a woman in black, heavily swathed in mourning veils who had stood out before her people there in Bucharest. Only later, looking backward, did the full omen of the event appear. At the time it seemed only that she was dressed as befitted the occasion, with the customary respect for that other from whose hand the sceptre had but just dropped.

King Carol's end had come quite without warning. There was no disease. It was his heart that had broken. Though a King of Roumania, he was still also a Hohenzollern of the Hohenzollerns. This his adopted country to which he had dedicated the earnest incessant toil of his lifetime had been upbuilded and restored through the support and influence of that other land of his birth. All of the industrial, commercial and educational connections he had so carefully welded were German in their origin. There was even a secret treaty which had bound Roumania in a political alliance with his dear fatherland. And Carol was of that stern virtue that had always made even his word as good as his bond. Now the war was turning the strongest, surest agreements into scraps of paper. It was when he knew with increasing certainty that the treaty he had made was not to be fulfilled, that he could no longer bear to live. On October 10, 1914, at Sinaia, he died.

It was in the night that it had occurred. In the

wide walnut bed in the great walnut room in which they slept at Castle Pelash, Elizabeth, "Carmen Sylva," the Queen, had suddenly awakened. There was a smothered exclamation she heard in the dark, "Oh, what is this!" And the man at whose side she had lain for forty years fell heavily across her. In vain her hand fumbled, fumbled for a bell she could not reach. And her husband lay a dead man in her arms. So they found him when they came at last in the morning.

The old King had not yet been placed in state on the catafalque when the Crown Prince and Princess, hastily summoned by telephone from Bucharest, arrived. Carmen Sylva was still sitting there in the bedchamber, a motionless figure clad in the symbols of mourning the ladies-in-waiting had brought for her costuming. Ferdinand went directly to his aunt and, controlling his own emotion, spoke to her comforting words.

It was Marie who dropped on her knees at the bed beside Uncle. They had not always agreed, the gay, bright Princess and the stern, severe, dead man. But beneath all their differences there had never failed the common bond of sympathy by which these two had always understood one another. Now the weeping woman realized how much she had loved him. It was her soul that sobbed itself out to his and to God. "O Lord," she prayed, "watch thou over the path in which thou hast this day set my feet. Perhaps thou hast ordained that it be neither short nor easy. But give me strength to face the future without fear or trembling." Then directly to Uncle she whispered a promise to carry on for the kingdom that had been his. It would not be in just his way. It would have to be in her way. But it would be all for the glory of his country, the good of his people, all for the Roumania they both held dear. It was with that promise, which Uncle now would more than ever understand, that Marie rose from her devotions by the dead man's side.

Directly to her own apartment she went to shut herself in alone with her sorrow. Soon there was a timid knock at her door. "Ninnie," the little Englishwoman who was her children's nurse, came tiptoeing in, and placed cool comforting hands on her throbbing brow as she lay there in her room where the shades were drawn.

"Your Majesty," said "Ninnie" softly. It was the first time the new title had been spoken. And she liked it that way. For one very near and of her own household, even as a nation the next day proclaimed, she was a Queen.

For three days the body of Carol reposed on the catafalque in the basilica of the monastery of Sinaia. For three days more at the Metropole in Bucharest he lay in state. Then they bore him to his final rest in another very old church, Curtea de Arges, where sleeps also its sixteenth century founder, Prince Magoe Bessarab and his wife Militza. Carmen Sylva returned to Sinaia to spend much time in the tiny but exquisitely beautiful chapel which years ago, at the death of her only child, she had arranged adjoining the great walnut bedchamber. Here before an embroidered altar, candle-lit and hung about with ikons, in an atmosphere all religiously rich in eastern coloring, she said her Lutheran prayers. And then, just about a year and a half later, she too was laid to her eternal rest beside her husband.

Immediately after the ceremony of installation at the Parliament House that day in 1914, the new King and Queen had gone in the afternoon to the Metropole for the Te Deum. And thereafter every little colorful church in the kingdom began celebrating the beautiful Flamanzi service with a revised "Mulzi ani Traiasca." Now the priest, holding aloft the silver cross, intoned: "For Ferdinand I King of Roumania, give, our Lord, long and happy days, success in his undertakings and over his enemies, victory. And let him live long years." From the choir-loft, peasant voices chanted in reply: "Long years may he live. God preserve him. God save him. God bless him." Again the priest lifted the silver cross and made petition for Marie, Queen of Roumania: "Let her live long years." And the choir chanted once more: "Long years may she live. God preserve her. God save her. God bless her."

So their reign began. And with this accession to the throne of the second generation of the dynasty, events arrived at a new turning point for this very ancient land. The signboard the Great War had set up in Europe pointed two ways. Which would be the winning way? One by one the nations had to choose. Roumania, between her old Latin origin and her new Teutonic affiliations, hesitated. The Central Powers were calling, threatening complete annihilation if she did not come. The Allies on the other side threatened too. But also they promised, if only she would be with them so that they need not be against her, marvelous prize of war. The country faced a crisis in which it might go down forever in oblivion, or rise in renown among the nations of the world. It was a woman who had the vision to see which way to go. As pro-German as had been the old King Carol, so pro-ally was the new Queen Marie.

Now all the batteries of their most suave diplomacy the Central Powers turned on her. It wasn't only politics and economics that they employed. Statecraft has more subtle methods than these. It was personality, the final most powerful appeal, they sought to use. There were ministers sent to the lady, oh most carefully selected ministers with the handsome eyes and the musical voice and the skill to say well the soft words a woman likes to hear. All the libations of their admiration they offered her. But never could they win the alliance that was sought. The lady only smiled and smiled and shook her head: "I am an English woman," always she answered steadily. "When Roumania comes into this war, there is but one side to choose."

Until Roumania was ready for that choice, the new Queen cleverly maneuvered. The country might become so almost evenly divided in sentiment that the balance of power would rest with the crown. For Ferdinand as naturally as for his predecessor, "Deutschland über alles," was the sure and firm tradition. For him, a Germany that would not win was unthinkable. "But we English," Marie insisted, "have built the world." To prove to him and to Roumania that England could not fail was the task that the granddaughter of Queen Victoria set for herself.

There were deputies and senators and statesmen and princes and generals she had over and again to tea. And the King of course three times a day at meals. When they brought her German victories, the Allied losses large in the newspaper headlines, she would always say: "Wait and see." And perhaps next day she presented them figures the other way about. Or if a German victory was real, then she played against it England's historic prestige and power. But when America, America, she held up to them, was coming in, she had them at grave attention.

When the Allies waxed warmer in overtures, with definite proposals of territory to be awarded in return for Roumania's assistance, she appealed to the national consciousness of the men about her. Had they not dreamed of lost dominions redeemed? And all those lands of their forefathers snatched through the centuries from the ancient

principalities of Wallachia and Moldavia, the
Allied armies were offering to recover and return
to them. For Transylvania, the Bucovina, the
Banat and Bessarabia, would they not join the Allied cause? It was a Roumania Irredenta she held
up to them. For two years they had been standing
neutral at the parting of the ways. But that time
was up. Now one side or the other would surely
compel them, she pointed out. And think of a
Greater Roumania! A Greater Roumania! They
thought, and all their Latin blood at last was up.

Ferdinand, it is true, was bound by every instinct and every tie to the race from which he had
sprung. But also he had sworn to be a Roumanian
King. And this was a country now calling to go
with its kind. Also this was not an absolute monarchy. He held his scepter not by divine decree
but by the will of the people whose best interests
he had given his sacred promise to serve. Torn between love and duty, the King was literally being
pulled up by the roots of all his traditions. He
could not sleep. In his agony he walked the floor
at night and tried to reach a decision. Could he
bring himself to declare for war against his own,
his dear fatherland? The Queen watched him
anxiously. She took him for long rides in the open
air of the countryside to revisit the scenes they had
loved when they were young. In late July they
were out one night like this. Their motor had
stopped while they silently watched the sun set
and the moon rise in the summer sky. A peasant

passed in the dusk. Shaking his head he muttered half to himself: "See the new moon. It's a red moon. A war moon."

And it was. On a day in August the King said: "I am ready for the Crown Council." The Queen nodded. So he summoned Roumania's statesmen. In the Council Chamber they took their seats about him, premier, ex-premiers, and ministers. With deep emotion, Ferdinand rose in his place to announce that the time had come for action: and for the realization of her national ideals, Roumania's advantage, he advised, lay in entering the war on the side of the Allies. He asked for the country's support in this course. By a vote of three quarters of its members, the Crown Council adopted the King's recommendation.

Outside a woman waited. "I had put the King into that room," she tells me to-day, "as if he were to have been delivered of a child. And I held my breath as eagerly for the news that it was successfully accomplished." When the door of the great state chamber opened and the nation's counselors filed out with their sovereign, it was the Queen who stepped to the King's side. One look into his face and she knew. She slipped her hand into his before them all. "Gentlemen," she said, "no one of you realizes so well as I what this has cost him. I am proud of him. And Roumania should be." So on August 27, 1916, Roumania entered the Great War.

And Marie came into her place in history. For

her personal charm and beauty, these her people
had acclaimed her as Queen of their hearts. Now
her personal leadership and courage of soul were
to make her in reality Queen of their country.
Military matters necessarily from now on would
occupy the attention of the King. For all other
matters it was going to come about that a people
in distress would turn to her. And a nation's
extremity was going to be her great opportunity.
Were they not already at the first call to the colors
hailing her as Empress!

At the railroad station in Bucharest where the
bands played and the flags waved, she had come to
bid Godspeed to those first troops off to the front.
As carload after carload of the youth of the land
pulled out, she, their sovereign, waved them on
their way. And she stood there in her beauty the
incarnation of their dreams, the symbol of their
national ideals for a Roumania redeemed. From
every train window they leaned out, waving back
to her with the one repeated cry: "Our Empress.
We shall make you Empress of all the Roumanians!" And she thrilled with pride perhaps not
unmixed with ambition.

A gift for ruling, you remember, she had by
natural inheritance. Statesmanship and politics
she had inevitably imbibed in the long, long talks
with which Uncle Carol had so bored her youth.
She had learned a good deal from him. Later
there had been all those pleasant hours in which
she was not so bored, passed by many ministers and

diplomats at the shrine of her presence: and she had learned still more from them. But to knowledge should be added understanding. Quite to clarify life, she must have also sorrow. None may so regally wear a crown as who first carries a cross. Well, her Calvary of suffering was very near.

At the railway station in Bucharest, soon the troop trains were coming back. There was no music now. And the flags were furled for shrouds. It was cargoes of the wounded and the dying they brought from the battlefields. The Queen stood by. "Oh," she cried, "what right have I to buy glory with the shedding of their blood? I feel so small, so humble before their stoic endurance." But she wore the uniform of a Red Cross nurse. And she too was giving, giving without stint of her endurance and magnificent physical strength for the country that she loved. As a Crown Princess, when in 1913 the Roumanian army had returned from a brief Balkan campaign and cholera had broken out, she had first learned to nurse the wounded. And it was that experience which was going to stand her in good stead now as she assumed the direction of the hospital work of a kingdom.

The bombs had begun to fall on Bucharest. On a single day hundreds of people lay dead and wounded in the streets. The Queen threw open the palace doors. "Bring them in," she called. And the royal residence was from then on a hospital. Soon every available building in Bucharest had been pressed into service to receive the wounded the trains were bringing from the front. From the country place outside the city to which the royal family had removed, the Queen came every day to make the rounds of the hospital wards. She brought delicacies to the men, kind words and her shining presence. To the other casualties of war were added the horrors of disease. Typhus and cholera raged. The typhus was carried by fleas and only one percent of the victims bitten and so infected ever recovered. But the Queen went straight ahead with her visitations to the hospitals where death was taking its increasing toll.

It was while engrossed like this with her patriotic devotion to other mothers' sons that what was perhaps the most severe test of soul that fate could find was preparing for Marie the Queen. She had, you see, a little son of her own, a darling, laughing baby. In a royal nursery, safeguarded by all the scientific care a kingdom afforded, he lived, you would have supposed, quite sheltered from all harm. And how it could have happened God alone knows. But when the pestilence and disease was at its height in the hospitals where the Queen went daily to nurse the soldiers, her own little Mircaea fell ill. He had typhoid which was followed by meningitis.

And it was while the little life hung in the balance that the German armies had crossed the Roumanian frontier. Onward they were marching straight toward Bucharest. And thicker and thicker above the doomed city, like awful birds of prey, dipped and swooped the Taubes and Zeppelins. But the baby Prince was now too ill to be removed to any safer refuge. In the immediate vicinity of the country residence that housed the royal family no less than seventy-two bombs fell in one night.

It was the night the Queen kept her vigil. But she hardly heard them. It was a terror much more subtle that tore at her heart. The child she held in her arms was slipping, slipping from her grasp. And she found herself as powerless as any lesser mother to hold him back. She too cried out her prayers to God to let her keep her son. And a whole nation was crying out for her and with her. Still, it could not be. And all the guards that barred the way were of no avail. In the darkness of that awful night, Death had entered the royal nursery. When morning dawned, the Queen was holding only a waxen-white little body that was but the empty casket from which her baby's soul had taken flight.

And boom, boom, boom, nearer and nearer came the cannon. Without burial pomp and ceremony and with only very simple prayers, they laid the little Mircaea in his tomb in the beautiful ancient basilica in the courtyard of the Cotroceni Palace, there at Bucharest. Nearer and nearer shrieked the guns while the Queen scattered white flowers above the marble slab that shut her baby in. Here you may read to-day an inscription: "In this sanctuary of Cotroceni, alongside of those who in former days were rulers of this land, lies the youngest son of King Ferdinand and Queen Marie born December 21, 1913. Mircaea died October 20, 1916, in the time of war, whilst the soldiers of Roumania were sacrificing their lives for the dream of centuries. Two years he remained sole guardian of the house of his parents over which his country's flag had ceased to float. Mourn for him for he shared with us the days of suffering: but the days of rejoicing he did not live to see."

Those words, however, had to wait to be inscribed until after the war was won. When the fall of the city was impending, there was no time to carve words in marble. With but a sobbing whispered farewell, Mircaea's mother had to leave him, her youngest and last born, her heart's dearest treasure to the mercy of an advancing foe.

The order had been given for the evacuation of Bucharest. The court and the government were to be transferred to Jassy. Very secretly, lest the Germans discover and attack them en route, the removal of the royal family had to be accomplished. They were conveyed in an automobile to a small station ten miles from Bucharest, and there placed aboard the train. All during the journey of that northward flight, the Queen sat with an open Bible on her knee. One had always been her favorite writer in that book, because he too was of royal birth and therefore had her own point of view on life. So now it was to the "words of the Preacher, the son of David, King of Jerusalem," that she had turned, as in her agony of soul she sought to fathom the ways of God. For she had been overwhelmed with resentment and with even amazement that anything so awful as this which had occurred could happen to her a Queen. Now in the beautiful soliloquy entitled Ecclesiastes, she read:

"That which is afar off and exceeding deep, who shall find it out? . . . I gave my heart to seek and search out by wisdom all things that are done under heaven. . . . I saw under the sun that the race is not to the swift nor the battle to the strong, neither yet bread to the wise man nor riches to men of understanding, nor yet favor to men of skill; but time and chance happeneth to all. . . . And I myself perceived that one event happeneth to them all."

Over and over that phrase echoed through the empty chambers of her heart: "One event happeneth to all." And at last she understood. In a moment of clarity, her royalty had shrunk to rags and she found herself completely kin to all the common people. "Thy son too shall be required of thee," God had proclaimed. So that she might better understand the tears of every mother. She dried her eyes. She refused to be broken by her personal grief. She put it aside that she might most effectively serve her people. From now on there was a new sweetness in her smile. And her heroism in the face of privations she shared for the sake of all those other mothers' sons, rose higher, ever higher.

At Jassy in old Moldavia in 1917, a nation stood at bay. Close to the trenches, the city had been selected as headquarters for the general staff and the temporary capital. As a university town it had accommodated a population of seventy thousand. Now there were a million people seeking shelter. On the train that brought them from Bucharest, the royal family lived three days before suitable living quarters could be arranged for them. Then a general gave up his house to the Queen and her children, and another small house was found for the King and his suite. And one of the gravest situations of the entire war closed down on the country.

It was never clear who had blundered. But the Allied assistance that was scheduled did not arrive. Little Roumania found herself fighting alone, cut off from those she had relied on as friends and at last almost completely surrounded by the enemy that had invaded her country. With a totally inadequate military equipment, with out-of-date guns and with none at all, sometimes with but their bare hands, the Roumanian army fought desperately on and hoped for relief by way of Russia. Up at Archangel were arriving food and munitions sent by the French and the English. But these supplies moved but slowly southward, large quantities accumulating in sheds at wayside stations all the way from Odessa to Jassy along the single line of communication, the Bessarabian railway that functioned with difficulty.

As for Russian troops, on a winter's night at Jassy from afar off was heard the tramp, tramp, tramp, of horses' hoofs. A premier's wife going home from a neighborhood call, turned to the maid who accompanied her: "What's that?" And soon by the light of the snow that covered the ground, they saw. Out of the darkness of the night came riding thousands of Cossacks clad in sheepskins and holding high lances.

"Ah thank God! But it is good you have come," cried Mme. Jonescu to the passing lines of riders.

And one laughed hoarsely. With a Russian voice, but in the Roumanian tongue, he called in reply: "No, it is not good we have come. We have had enough of fighting."

Which was advance information of the forthcoming Russian revolution. Small wonder it was that Russian coöperation now was but half-hearted and of almost no avail. Practically alone, the brave Roumanian army made that stand against the Central Powers which was of so much assistance to the Allied cause in that it engaged the attention of powerful German divisions who were thus diverted from damage elsewhere. There came a French mission of some five hundred officers and also a smaller British delegation to assist in the rebuilding of the shattered Roumanian army. And then was won the brilliant victory over Mackensen at

Marasheshti in a line of battle that extended from Bucharest to Jassy. But of course with obsolete weapons and with no adequate support by way of relief, the Roumanians in the long run were waging a losing fight. Their soldiers were mowed down like grain. In that awful winter of 1917 alone, two hundred and fifty thousand had fallen in battle and one hundred thousand persons had been swept away in the plague of disease.

It was the coldest winter in fifty years. And everything required for supporting existence was lacking. In the awful crisis that the country faced a woman was doing what she could. Food was scarce and wood was scarcer. Even the royal family did not know from dinner to dinner what there would be to eat on the morrow. The household of one of the ladies-in-waiting existed for months on beans. In the people's desperate situation it was the Queen whose unflinching courage kept the national spirit alive. No occasion was too trivial and none too difficult for her personal attention and resourcefulness. When the Mayor of Jassy was unable to get the snow removed from the streets by the wholly exhausted and half dead men available for the purpose, it was the Queen who came out to lead them and the work was done. When complete famine threatened the city, it was she who sent private motor cars scouring the country for flour and organized the bakeries of Jassy.

But details like these to which she turned on call never interrupted her larger work. Sewing machines set up at the royal residence itself were turning out rapidly garments and sheets and pillow cases for hospital supplies. The Princesses Elisabeta and Mignon had been trained for service. Even the little Princess Ileana was helping, going about with her mother to carry thermos bottles of hot tea to men who lay dying in the streets of the city and along the country roads. And regularly the Queen was going the rounds of hospitals not so easy to reach as those first opened in Bucharest. They were scattered now through the mountains and over the Moldavian plains. Right at the front had been organized the Regina Maria hospital with hundreds of beds. Four more field hospitals had been added to it and three movable hospitals were set up, all of these bearing Her Majesty's name and all under her direct personal oversight.

But no hospital was too hard for her to visit. Where the railroad did not run or the royal automobile could not go, she went on horseback. Even also right to the front and under shrapnel fire she insisted on going to inspect the troops and cheer the men in the trenches. Through the plague, pestilence and death that now swept the country, she the Queen went everywhere undaunted. Alike fearless of the bullets falling at the front and the terrible filth and disease she faced in the overcrowded hospitals, she went indefatigably on with her war work. "Where my soldiers are," she said, "there I may not hesitate to be."

Always like that, smiling and unafraid, she en-

tered a ward with its long line of cots. From all
the sights and sounds of suffering she did not flinch.
With her own hands she smoothed softly the hands
that had fought for her throne. With her own
handkerchief she wiped the cold dew of agony
from the brow of many a boy. She touched and
caressed so tenderly. And "Where does it hurt
the most?" she'd ask. And "Tell me all about it,"
she'd urge. And she listened. Oh, how she listened!

Scarcer and ever scarcer were supplies. But
the Queen struggled desperately to have the few
little luxuries she brought the men as gifts. Her
sympathy and her chocolates and her cigarettes
could sometimes do more than drugs. The delicacies that she gave out with her own hands were
carried in a basket by an aide-de-camp who followed in her wake. And the man for this service
had to be carefully selected. Could he endure the
hospital smells? From the most terrible fetid
odors the Queen herself never drew back. No
faintest expression of repugnance marred the look
of divine compassion with which she bent above
a bed of pain. Nothing ever stopped her. Before the door of a hospital for the hopelessly in-
curable typhus cases, a doctor one day barred her
way. "Your Majesty," he begged, "there's no need
of going in there. They're all dying, and it's too
dangerous."

"Dying?" said the Queen. "Then it's my duty."
As she crossed the threshold, the first sound to

reach her ears was the delirious cry of a dying soldier calling for his wife. "Here, dear, here I am," answered Her Majesty, walking directly to his bedside. She knelt down and folded him close to her heart. And as she soothed him so, he smiled and closed his eyes, and died happily in her arms.

You see how it was always without any least reservation that she gave herself, fully, fearlessly, joyously. Fortunate it was that she was a woman who, in the sheltered days gone by, had lived with an eager zest for all the gaiety her carefree world could give her. So she had stored up, as it were, a splendid reserve power. She had, you see, an already sunlit spirit to light her on her way through the darkness and desolation where now she walked. Suffering and misery were everywhere literally overwhelming the stricken land. The hospitals were spilling over: three men in one bed and long lines of ambulances arriving with others waiting in anguish for those to die and give their places. There was not lumber enough to build barracks to shelter these ever multiplying, waiting wounded. There were not even boards enough to make coffins for the dead. And worse, now there were not drugs and anæsthetics with which to treat those still alive; paper swabs and sawdust were being used for dressings.

When the American Red Cross and the Y.M.C.A. arrived bringing first aid, it was a woman with eager outstretched hands who welcomed them. "Over the sights that you will see," she said, "and my cruel impotence to help, my heart has been breaking." But before the people she had kept her courage always high. She was to them the Universal Mother. Literally "Mother of all" was what they were calling her.

And it was to Her Majesty that the relief workers, even as the rest of the world around her, now turned for direction. Along the roads of death their motor cars went piled, with the provisions and supplies they had brought for distribution. And always the royal motor led all the rest. When the roads became impassable and they had to walk, a Queen walked with them. To the hillside dugouts that served as hospitals, to far, pest-infected little villages, she led the way. Other welfare workers wore out. But she went on. When there were those who urged that she spare herself, she shook her head: "I have health and vigor which God has given me for a purpose. It must not be wasted. Because I cannot help but feel strong, I must work to win." Men finally were assigned in relays to keep up with her. There was a Virginia gentleman whose strength struggled to match his devotion. And indeed he never gave up. But his personal chauffeur came one day to him. "Maybe you can stand the pace, sir. But I can't," declared the man, and resigned his job. The Queen, however, never weakened. Day after day from nine in the morning till seven-thirty at night, she did not falter or stop. And weeks went by like that. And months.

Then it was a very brave lady who had faced death and disaster. Could she now bear defeat? The enemy were cruelly battering down the country's last power of resistance. In spite of the victory that had halted Mackensen, three-fourths of the nation's territory was now in the hands of the Germans. All merely first-aid efforts would no longer avail to hold Roumania up. But who would break the truth to the Queen? Not a general would. Not the King himself would. They finally sent an Englishman to tell her. She flung back her head: "But why should we give up? Because we are a small nation, are we less brave than England? And England never gives up."

Gently, very gently but very firmly, her own countryman at last made plain the truth. Eight hundred thousand Roumanian soldiers were dead. And it was useless to send to sacrifice and death the rest of the Roumanian army. Then a woman wept. It was Mircaea's mother. And her weeping was terrible. For the tears she shed were for all those other mothers' sons who had died for Roumania.

There had to be made the armistice with the Germans. The Queen was obliged to receive at her house the German general who took over Jassy. It was a white-faced woman who came down the staircase. On the last stair she stood. She did not extend her hand. The officer who looked at her and bowed was trembling too. She made some necessary perfunctory remark: "Did he find himself comfortably housed?" And the audience was over.

Now there were the farewells to her friends. All American, English and French were under military orders to depart. Officers, doctors and relief workers of the Allies who had been with her for eighteen months came to say good-by. An American there was who gripped her hand in emotion; but it was not enough and he fell on his knees to kiss the hem of her dress. It was to a Frenchman she herself said with a smile that flashed whimsically through her pain and suffering, "General, couldn't you give me the accolade?" And she found herself caught to an ample breast and kissed on both cheeks. Some one, it must have been a Frenchman too, saluted and said: "You are the flag we have planted in this soil we have been defending with you. Stand steadfast. Be strong. And we shall come back." An Englishman called her "the flame of resistance that no storm could put out." Like that, reluctantly they had to leave her, the woman they all longed to defend. Then the Roumanians came to her and said in their despair, "Everything is over." But they added "However, we still have you." Against all the darkness which in that March, 1918, had descended on a nation, she indeed in her brave beauty stood out a compelling figure. And who shall say how much that may have contributed to the final denouement? Here is a woman for whom men singly or in armies ever would be happy to fight.

And one remained with her to the end. When the Germans had ordered all the Allies out, a Canadian colonel did not go. Soon the Bolsheviki of Russia had declared war on Roumania and were fighting for the supplies which were on the way down through Bessarabia. All transports now practically ceased. Only the Canadian colonel was able to negotiate with the Bolsheviki for such supplies as finally reached Jassy. And now indeed did the Roumanian cause look lost. See how the sky of hope was all overcast. Terrible things began to happen in Russia. Roumania lay so near, right in the very shadow of them. Suppose the shadow moved southward? To her people then the Queen could only say heroically: "Whatever is to be will be. We are in the hands of God."

But she never flinched, even though personal grief was added to her national anxiety as history moved inexorably. For her it was more than an Empire and a court that had fallen up there. It was the land and the house of her Russian forebears. Where she remembered so well the glint of gold and precious stones, the shine of old ikons, diademed women with gleaming shoulders and men in gorgeous uniforms, where all these had been were now palace halls run red with their blood. More than a Czar and his nobles had been removed. For her it was a cousin, and men and women she called intimately by their first names, who had been murdered. She covered her face with her hands when she thought of Nicky with his dreamy gray-brown eyes and with his delicately modelled lips that were shaped for soft words only. A fair, gentle-faced youth he had been at his crowning, entering into the mighty inheritance of the ages that had now swept him out of existence. Even her own sister, together with husband and family, had narrowly escaped annihilation. It was her dearest sister, Ducky, Victoria Melita, who was married to the Grand Duke Cyril Vladimirovitch, now that the rest were dead, who was the next in direct succession to the Russian throne. The Grand Duke and the Grand Duchess and the Princess Mashka and another daughter had all been lined up against a wall while the Bolshevik soldiers debated whether to shoot or not to shoot, and decided to leave it for another day. In that interval of chance the family had succeeded in fleeing to Switzerland. En route, in Finland, a little son was born to the Grand Duchess who had no layette. The Queen sent to her sister all of Mircaea's baby clothes.

While horrors like these swept her heartstrings at Jassy, all the lesser little annoyances of existence too harassed her days. Each of the children in turn had to have the jaundice. And when she was busiest with the sorrows and cares of a nation it was then that Carol had slipped away from his regiment to his romance with Zizi Lambrino. The Queen went with her motor car up to the Russian border to bring him back. "Now," she said

wearily to a friend, "I feel like an old woman."
But that too passed. Again she flung high her
head as her country called her. The peace treaty
with the Germans that was to have followed the
armistice she had delayed and delayed by one
ruse and another. Now again a crisis threatened.
The Crown Council at last seemed about to accede
to the peace, and the Queen, a woman, could not
enter their Council Chamber. She sent her son
instead. "I know," she said to Carol, "it's going to
be hard for you to stand up against your father
and all the rest. But you must. Just rise in your
place and say that you are speaking with a message from me and from all the mothers of Roumania: tell them that not for a German peace have
the women of Roumania given their sons to die
for their country." So Carol did.

And the peace wasn't signed that day. It never
was officially finished, so that it has gone down in
history only as the "mock peace." Just before its
completion might have been finally forced, Allied
assistance arrived. "It all seemed incredible. The
end came with such a rush. We were hardly able
to grasp it all," the Queen said in a far-away reminiscent voice, as she told me about it in the high-
towered golden room at the castle in Sinaia.

Those gallant Frenchmen did, you see, come
back. And English troops too. The German in-
vaders who had held this land so mercilessly in
their grasp were vanquished and obliged to with-
draw in defeat. And it was a lady very beautiful

and fair who together with her nation had been delivered from distress.

On that great day in the autumn of 1918, when the Roumanian army triumphantly returned with the French and English troops to take possession once more of Bucharest, they marched down the city's historic Avenue of Victory, the Calea Victorei. And at the head of the troops on prancing horses there were three who rode abreast: King Ferdinand, General Berthelot of France and Marie, the Queen of Roumania.

How the people cheered: Maria Regina! Maria Regina!

CHAPTER X

The "Luck of the Country"

IT was indeed a surprising occurrence. But the peasant deputies, when they had recovered from their wonder, were really more pleased than otherwise. Only the senators of old Boyar descent were plainly perturbed at a proceeding so at variance with established order in this part of the world. In 1919 the first Parliament of the new Roumania had been opened with benefit of a woman's presence. It had been convened by the King and the Queen together. And this is the form which has been ever since observed.

The innovation had followed a declaration to the ministers. "I have," the Queen told them, "given this country six children. I have been your inspiration and mainstay through the war. Now it seems no longer fitting that I sit in a box in the background at the opening of Parliament. I wish to stand side by side with the King when His Majesty assembles the government."

"But," they had protested in consternation, "it's not a woman's place. Nothing like that has ever been done in Roumania." They were talking, however, to a lady who has discovered that many a thing which has not been done should be. Particularly was she firm about this. The Premier, who had been a General, at length agreed with her. And to her statesmen, yielding with anxious solemnity, the Queen had retorted blithely: "You'll always now and then have to shudder a bit at the very unusual things I shall do."

That same year, white bullocks, to the accompaniment of sacred ceremony, plowed the first furrows in execution of Roumania's new agrarian law. And there was another historic achievement. Marie packed her trunks for Paris and picked up from the Peace Conference the Greater Roumania which the world now sees outlined on the map of Europe.

On each of these occasions there were those among her Government and her aristocracy whom the Queen had been obliged to remind: "You'll always now and then have to shudder a bit at the very unusual things I shall do. But," she assured them, "if I shock you sometimes, well, you will shudder for only a comparatively short space of time as outlined against the centuries. And I shall look the other way not to be bothered by your disturbance. Meanwhile, I shall have accomplished for Roumania that which will endure for future generations."

It has already made Stefan Boerescu a happy man. Where once he owned two acres of land now he owns twenty or thirty. I think last spring he made it forty. In the principalities of Moldavia and Wallachia alone there are one million six hundred and fifteen thousand, three hundred and three other peasant farmers just as happy as Stefan, because their holdings have been similarly and proportionately increased. In old Roumania before the war there were some four thousand of the great Boyars who used to hold three-fifths of all the arable land, the remaining two-fifths being all there was left to go round among the more than a million and a half small farmers like Stefan. So that some had only two or three acres and some even owned no land at all. How, then, could they live? Well, as Stefan did, by hiring out on the great estates.

Prince Ricka used to pay Stefan only one and one-half lei a day. Still there was nowhere else to turn for employment, no factory in the next village, no stores along its curving crooked street. This is an agricultural country where 80%, to be exact 82%, of the population live in rural communities and must make their living from land, either their own or another's. So powerful is the person holding vast acres of it, that though titles were in Roumania officially abolished in 1866, he can scarcely lose his and is usually yet saluted as Prince. Land, therefore, you can see, literally means life and liberty to live it.

The peasant's hope for having land had been always as cherished a dream as his hope for heaven. And it had been just as far away, because even if he could have earned the money to pay for it, there was no land to be bought. So valued was it that it passed always on in the family from father to son. None was ever sold. And the peasant lived always with his longing for land. He wanted land that he might have life, and have it more abundantly, more mamaliga, more milk and cheese, more leisure.

There was once a Queen who did not understand why people should want more than they have. And she made a terrible historical mistake when she querulously inquired, "If they haven't got bread, why don't they eat cake?"

But the Queen of Roumania now isn't at all that kind of Queen. She has, you see, looked through the lighted windows of life. Not for nothing had the Crown Princess Marie ridden out and away from the Court to find the hearts and the homes of these, her people. So well she knew in how many cottages there was tuberculosis. So well she knew how many babies the women had borne and how many buried in a national infant mortality rate that mounted to 60%. And she had come to palace halls fortified with an awakened knowledge that was to be a surer protection than any ancient outworn defenses against the dangers that may beset a throne and a realm to-day, even as in the days when that other less fortunate Queen lost hers.

For however those about Marie of Roumania might patter their pleasant platitudes, out there just across the royal horizon, she had seen where there was distress and misery and sorrow in daily life. And she had not missed its meaning. Somehow the word of the Lord had come unto her that the earth and the fullness thereof can no longer be the divine right of any group or class. How it could have happened one may not say, except that she is a twice born soul and so knows how to listen. But as surely as to David or Solomon or any of those royalties of old, God had spoken also to this modern sovereign.

And the first pronouncement of the new Queen of Roumania was that the people must have land. Where should it come from? Why, from those who already had too much of it, the great Boyars. But these, the lords of the realm, would not wish to give up their ancestral acres. No? Then the land would have to be taken from them. How? Ah, that was the agrarian question.

And something like this spoke the Queen: Whether you wish it or not, my friends, the world must change. It is still in the hands of the potter, who is shaping human destiny. Nothing is permanent and established—not even the seats of the mighty perhaps. What is to be one may not know. Only that to-morrow will not be as to-day. And that to-day there must be doing. Shall it be by peaceful process in conformity with God's law of growth? Or if we defy that law, shall it then be through a social order crushed and ground beneath the Juggernaut of progress, so to rise again? A teakettle boils quite serenely if you let the lid lift gently. But if you hold down the lid, you may get an explosion.

It had been that Crown Princess who rode out on horseback who had first heard the kettle boiling. And she had rushed back to the palace to give the alarm. Otherwise, Uncle Carol, sitting always there at his great carved desk, might never have known. As she left the royal presence he had murmured, as once before: "Good stuff in that girl."

A little later, by long slow constitutional amendment, Parliament in Roumania had begun to move toward agrarian reform. It had not yet been achieved, however, when Ferdinand came to the throne. As it lingered, the war had intervened. At last it was the Queen who came to the King and the ministers with the warning that they must not wait. "Listen!" she said. And they too could hear the slogan the Liberal party was calling even above the battlefields: "The land belongs to him who tills it."

Even at Jassy then the agrarian measure was written. Four people framed it, the King and the Queen, the King's wisest councilor and the Liberal party's political leader. "Oh," gasped the Boyars when the rumor had reached them, "the King and the Queen are in the hands of the Liberals." "But no," Her Majesty had replied, "the King and the Queen are leading the Liberals."

At Bucharest, as soon as the government had

returned in December, 1918, the first bill to be
presented for passage by the Roumanian parliament was the agrarian measure with its proposal
for a new allotment of the lands of a kingdom.

"Ours, the Crown Lands, shall be the first to
go," pledged the King, stepping out before the
people. And it was 150,000 hectares, 375,000
acres, of waving grain fields that he surrendered.

"Yours, too," called the House of Deputies to
the nobles. And an angry aristocracy rose in
protest.

"Hark!" commanded the Queen. Just beyond
the Dniester revolution rumbled. Over the border came the boom, boom, boom, of Bolshevik
guns.

Only the Queen was smiling, as ever cool and
unafraid. She nodded. "You have heard? But
it need not happen here. We can build our ram-
parts high against it. Only you'll have to throw
in your wealth like sand."

Now, no one hated more than she to see her
wheat fields go—and the power and prestige which
belonged with the possession of vast landed estates. But her lifted vision is toward the future.
Again she spoke: "Gentlemen, the earth moves.
We may put to the rack and the inquisition those
who say it does. Every age has done that with its
seers. And the blood of the martyrs is the seed of
revolution. Better it is to look the truth in the
face. Do not dare defy it. On the altars of new
truth disclosed to the heart of man, every age must

make its sacrifice. I'll walk right up and make mine. I've no intention of being dragged by the hair of my head to be cast thereon."

Then, "Hurry!" called the Queen to Parliament. It did. With a rush, the agrarian measure was made the agrarian law. By its provisions no one in all Roumania, in either the ancient provinces or the new ones so recently acquired, may now retain more than a maximum of 1,250 acres of arable land. All the rest must be given up. In lots of thousands of acres, sometimes ten thousand, sometimes twenty thousand, even sixty thousand acres and more, the Boyars of Roumania have brought the vast holdings of their landed estates to have the titles rewritten in the new names of millions of peasants.

And this is the way it was arranged. A state commission of engineers was sent out in each Principality to make what was called the cadastral survey. Just how much land there was and where situated went on record for the entire country. There was an official valuation. The proprietors were not required to give up the land without indemnity, but it was obligatory that they accept the price which the government fixed. And payment was made by the Ministry of Finance in government bonds. All of the hundreds of thousands of acres thus acquired by the state were now laid out in small plots of five hectares, about twelve acres each. These were sold to the new peasant proprietors at just half the price the government had paid the original owners, the other half being charged up to be paid from the national taxes. To make it possible for every one to share in the land division, the easiest terms were arranged for the new proprietors: only 20% of the purchase price was required in cash, the remainder to become due in annual installments over a period of twenty years.

Well, a new Magna Charta for human liberty had been written. And it was way down there where East meets West in a land at least a hundred years away. A nation came stepping upward out of feudal custom that had clung to it like a garment, though federal form had of course in fact been already established in 1854. And the people in their joy must make holiday of the new occasion. So in every commune, the land sale, the inpropriation, as it is called, has been inaugurated with a festival.

See how it happens. The people have come out in all their brilliant embroideries. The women are wearing their golden *salbas*. The men have put the peacock feather in their hats. The gypsy musician, the *lautari,* has brought his *cobsa* with which to make melody. There is a two hours' program of glad speechmaking and picturesque ceremony. A government minister who has come from Bucharest makes the address which presents the land to the people. Then the white bullocks are led out, the great majestic creatures which, next to land itself, are a peasant's dearest possession. The most beautiful ones the country affords have been selected, with the widest branching horns. There are ten of them hitched to a plow all festooned with flowers. The priest in glittering vestments comes with holy water. There is a solemn breathless hush that betokens the gratitude to God felt by the entire assemblage. The priest has made a libation, sprinkling the plow with the holy water. It is now the priest who first turns a few furrows. Then the minister from Bucharest takes the plow. Then each of the local officials have rolled up some of the fragrant brown earth. There are more speeches.

The program closes with the singing of the national anthem. O, hear it ring out: "Awake, Roumania, from the sleep of death which for centuries hath enchained thee." And if you listen very softly, from the Carpathian mountains you may catch an echo mingled with far away undertones of the Marseillaise and the Star Spangled Banner. In old Moldavia, in France or in the United States of America, there is a brotherhood of the human spirit that thrills through the ages.

Stefan has been so happy with his land since he got it that it has been difficult to get him to leave it. A peasant with his ground about him is like an artist with a new canvas and a box of paints. All the artistry of Stefan's soul was aglow as his little plot came out in the colorful picture of his skillful plant arrangement. So absorbed was he in this, his own creative effort, that when the call came for laborers on Prince Ricka's estate, he said he couldn't go. So many others said this, too, that in a little while the superintendent returned with special inducements. It used to be, you remember, that the wages for labor on the great estates were one and one-half lei a day. Well, now Prince Ricka would pay five lei a day. Still Stefan would not go. But for five lei a day he would send his wife. Often she had gone to the great house as an extra housemaid. She could work as well in the fields. And the leis she earned they put in a stocking.

The next year the superintendent came very earnestly asking for Stefan: a man was better than a woman. If Stefan himself would come, it would now be ten lei a day. That was a good deal of money. So Stefan did go. And the leis he earned were put in the stocking.

But not all the laborers who were bidden would come. Even the wives that some promised to send didn't come. So many in fact failed altogether that much of the harvest on the big estate could not be gathered at all. The next year wages went to twenty lei a day and Stefan's stocking jangled full. But still not enough men could be had and, for the lack of them, the Boyars' crops rotted on the ground. Well, wiser than that it would be to cultivate less. Before the following spring, Prince Ricka, out of the 1,250 acres the government had permitted him to retain, was offering 400 for sale. And out came Stefan's leis. Five hectares more of land he bought, and now he had eleven. My, but that was quite a little estate, over 27 acres, and he was very busy. So busy indeed that when Prince Ricka's superintendent came for summer labor, he couldn't possibly go. No, not even his wife, for she, too, was needed now on their own acres. Well, but for, say, thirty lei a day? Yes, for so much as that perhaps Stefan could spare a little of his time.

Now, that is the way that wages have gone up and up. How much do you suppose a man is worth to-day in Roumania? As much as sixty, seventy, even eighty lei a day, Stefan has been offered for his labor. And still labor is scarce and the crops lie on the ground on the big estates and cannot be gathered. And always the great proprietors are compelled to sell more of their dwindling holdings. Four hundred acres more Prince Ricka sold two years ago. And always the more the peasants buy, the busier they are at home and the higher go the wages to get them away. The stockings fill up to bursting with leis.

Last spring a delegation from the village at the gates of his estate waited on Prince Ricka. No, they said, the superintendent wouldn't do. They would see the Prince himself. They did.

The spokesman was Stefan's brother-in-law, Vasili Moruzi, who had worked in the steel mills in Youngstown, Ohio. Vasili hadn't been quite the same since he had come back. It is said they are never quite the same. In almost every com-

mune now you may find them, these men whom the
war called back from maybe Paterson, N. J., or
from Youngstown, Ohio, before they had completed American citizenship. And they have returned to the old world homeland with new world
ideas. The father of this peasant Vasili kissed
the feet of Prince Ricka's father. He himself
used always to kiss the Prince's hand. Now he
only stood respectfully, with his cap removed.
And Stefan and all the others in line behind him,
were doing just as he did. He would have shaken
hands: but the Prince had missed the gesture. So
the man began very simply and straightforwardly.
"We have come, Sir," he said, "because we would
like some more land." The Prince's face stiffened.
And Vasili hastened to add: "We would say it
only very gently. We mean no harm. But we
now have the money, and we should like to buy
some more land."

"But," retorted the Prince, "have I not already
sold so much that I have not enough left from
which to live! What shall I myself do when I
have sold you all my land?"

"That is easy," answered Vasili, who had been
in Youngstown, Ohio. "In America the great
Boyars do not keep the land. They themselves go
to work in offices and stores and manufactories."

And even so, just that they are beginning to do
in Roumania. Not the aged Prince Ricka, of
course. He went now angrily inside his house and
closed the door. But his son has gone already

256

from the idle leisure class to employment in a bank in Bucharest. The young man went sadly, though resignedly. At one of the great Roumanian country houses where I was a guest with the Queen, a gentleman who could speak English was kindly interpreting to me my environment. About the young Prince who sat across the table, he lowered his voice as he explained: "He works, poor fellow; clerk for a lumber company." There was compassionate sympathy in the gentleman's voice for the calamity which had overwhelmed his friend. And that is the way all the first families feel when they find their sons forced out in the world to earn a living.

But it has to be faced at last, that the diminished acres of the former great estates no longer afford an income adequate for the accustomed style of ease and grandeur. The lord of the manor can no longer maintain a residence in Bucharest and another in Paris. Even with the best yield of corn and wheat, the cost of the labor to harvest it has so cut down the net income that a Boyar is fortunate to get enough with which to meet household expenses on the ancestral estate. He may have to sell and move to a "flat" in one of the apartment buildings now going up in Bucharest. Or, if he struggles on with country life, he must let its luxury go. So all of the rushing gaiety in which the Roumanian aristocracy once lived is muted to a simplicity of existence that seems spare indeed.

And it is accepted, to say the least, with hurt surprise.

Prince Ricka's wide white house had for four hundred years echoed with the hospitality here dispensed, when haughty ladies and gentlemen of high lineage ate and drank and made merry beneath this roof. But now silver plate and ancestral china stand in long rows, shut within glass cabinets seldom opened. In cobwebbed cellars wait old wines for which no revellers now call. In the elegant drawing-rooms, rich rare rugs and marvelous tapestries are mellowing in the dust. Up in the great ball room to which two spiral staircases ascend from the main hall below, gilded mouldings are tarnishing and crystal chandeliers are dim: not since the war has been heard here the sound of the *cobsa* and the violin. In their painted portraits all through the house, turbaned ancestors look from the walls in wonder at these silent ways. All the rooms seem ghostly with guests gone by. Only an occasional servant slips along the corridors; where once there were fifteen or twenty, now there are only five.

Outside, one very old liveried retainer still bows low at the entrance gate to the motor car that sweeps up the long avenue of lime trees. In the waxen green vineyards, a watchman wearing at his waist the polished horn of a bullock on which to sound an alarm, guards the blue and gold and purple fruit. The gardens, the amazing gardens that stretch in such colorful carpets of beautiful bloom, are yet for a little while weeded by patient fingered girls on their knees. One, there, is Stefan's daughter. Oh, these Roumanian gardens, broad fields of heliotrope purpling fragrantly into ageratum's soft lavender; sunny stretches of marigold deepening down to nasturtiums' copper velvet; pink verbenas pressing to beds spilled red with geraniums; and always like this, the color laid on in wave after wave, swirling lavishly. Not in Elysian fields or on Olympian heights, I am sure, will you come upon color rioting so gloriously, so gorgeously.

These Roumanian gardens! And must these, too, pass with the pleasure people who paid for them? Let even social progress pause an instant, poignant pain at the heart. But the times are inexorable. Already the great estates are wrecked and fortunes cut in little pieces. Labor is asking more leis, always more and more leis, and chicken for the menu in the servants' dining room. Even though you give them what they want, they are not easy to get. Stefan's wife now stops at home. Soon will Stefan's daughter. And servants' manners towards their betters are no longer nice. They do not always kiss the hand.

So the white-haired Prince Ricka has slammed the door of his house. He has gone inside with his despair. "Life is finished," he bitterly declares. "Let the world go past outside. All of this horrible new Democracy I do not understand."

Ah, how should he? With all the formal beauty

of ancient birthright fading about him. With a glittering past going out in gathering shadow.

But it is Stefan who stands at the dawn. At his house now see the cow where they used to have but a goat. Such delicious milk there is for the children's mamaliga. In the dooryard a pig fattens: there is going to be meat for the table. Last year there was built a new room on the little thatched cottage: three rooms there are now instead of the two. It is much better for five children that they have more air and more space in which to live the long winter that wraps all about so white and so tight beneath the snow. So much there is one may do with money; the new phonograph that stands beneath the ikon's sacred niche, it is to the children so great a wonder.

Everything, too, gets to be now so nice and easy. Work that was once an ache in the back to a man comes not that way with the machine. It used to be in Roumania that only the great estates had machinery for farming. It cost, of course, too much for little ones. And then too it was strange and foreign; Stefan, along with the others, used to stand around jeeringly exultant at the experts who had to be so often summoned to make the wheels go round. But now something very interesting has happened. Stefan's brother-in-law has been satisfied to stop with five hectares of land, and with the rest of his leis has bought a threshing machine. With it he goes about from place to place and he says: "If you have a hundred bushels of wheat, I will thresh it for you if you give me seven." It was at the government's experimental farm he learned how to operate the machine so that it does not break down.

Everything that anybody in the world knows about machines and about plants they can tell you there at the new state farm. Some forty-eight of these farms the government has opened throughout Roumania. The celebrated director of plant industry, Dr. D. L. Andronescu, himself a descendant of the old nobility, has his Ph.D. degree from the University of Illinois. How great is that institution nobody can tell quite so well as a Roumanian peasant who has once been a laborer in the steel mills at Youngstown, Ohio. Always as his countrymen gather around to hear, Vasili puffs out his chest. And in America, he declares, no man cuts grain with a scythe or threshes it out with a hand flail.

Well, in Roumania, too, some day soon it will be like that. Already there is such a demand for machinery for the new small farms that a new way has been found to get it: some of the villages now have the "coöperative," an organized group which owns the machinery passed around in turn for the use of its members. They buy seed, too, at wholesale and together market their produce at advantageous prices. No less than six hundred and ninety-eight of these coöperatives are listed throughout Roumania.

Hear the Roumanian monastery bells ringing

the Angelus of a new civilization. Oh, wasn't it well when a Queen beat her peoples' swords into plowshares, and bade a prostrate peasantry rise?

It was after the harvest last fall that Stefan took his family for a trip to Bucharest. Two nights and a day they were on the road. The white oxen traveled leisurely. But everybody was very comfortable on the straw in the wagon with the thatch-covered top. And they were very much excited. For the first time in their lives they were going to a moving picture; it was the "Covered Wagon," brought all the way from America. I saw the Boerescus in Bucharest coming down the Calea Victorei, the white oxen stepping solemnly. Something caught in my throat. Why, see here, pioneering Roumanian peasants in their covered wagon catching up with ours! For they too face the wide new spaces in life.

How far, I wonder, will this new covered wagon be going? Already in Roumania they have their new rights of man through evolution instead of revolution. There is a printed government report that reads: "What would have happened without the agrarian reform, and what a repercussion the putting off of the same might have provoked throughout Europe, are hypotheses which we would rather not consider."

Three Empires, you see, already have crumbled across this country's very boundary lines. A Czar of Russia has been destroyed. A Kaiser of Germany has been dethroned. An Emperor of Austria has resigned. A King of Greece has retired. And other thrones are rocking.

But now watch Roumania's covered wagon. Can it be they may pass even ours on the road of progress? For there is more to the agrarian measure way down there than on the surface alone appears. There is more than Stefan's farm. The Queen has a land law really deeper than any that's been done before. It was written with a vision of the future and wonders that may be, which only the great prophets in political economy have glimpsed. Here, if you please, is a country with vast mineral deposits and some of the richest oil fields of Europe within its domains: and by the agrarian law all sub-soil rights have been reserved to be vested in the state, that is to say, in the people!

Why, to-day, around the world, is the echo of a woman's wit. It is indeed to laugh. In vain let the foreign speculators and profiteers rage. At the hotel Athenee Palace in Bucharest, they are always from all lands arriving. And always Ali the imperturbable, at Bar Americaine, is called on to administer the whisky and soda or the Manhattan cocktail to alleviate their chagrin. Loudly they call on their consulates and their embassies. Come the greatest ministers to Cotroceni Palace to kiss the hand of Queen Marie and bespeak for the powerful money interests of their homelands her favor. But always they must leave, hat in hand. "Go tell your governments, gentlemen," she replies, "how much we'd like your financiers' assistance in the development of our natural resources. But it will have to be on our terms. Not fifty million dollars, nor two hundred and fifty million, will tempt me to part with any of the possessions of my people. All sub-soil rights here remain vested in the Roumanian state."

The official record for the Roumanian oil wells in May, 1926, was a production of 268,036 tons. In April, 1925, the foreign trade deficit was 722,-000,000 lei. In April, 1926, the deficit had been converted into a surplus of 560,000,000 lei. And now when the Queen of Roumania stands beside the King for the opening of Parliament, her statesmen nod to each other. "She's the luck of the country," they say, "the luck of the country!"

But there is more. Really, the lady has confounded the diplomacy of our day. With all the witching ways of a woman, she combines a vision so astute that no statesman may surpass it. It was at the Peace Conference where she played the part that stirred the world to the wonder of her genius. I know of no one who went away from Paris with more satisfactory annexations than did Marie of Roumania.

Not, of course, that hers were so much in the way of winnings as great nations picked up for themselves at the Peace Table. But this was a little nation. And consider its gains proportionately: was there any other country that doubled a domain? Nor had the lady been expected to be among those present at Versailles.

You see, it had been when the conflict was raging that nations had called in their agony, Women wanted! But after the war was won, and men would make the peace, this they decided they'd do alone. And it was all of the wisest men from every land who were gathered there at Paris finishing off the war they had made, settling up the affairs of civilization. Hardly had the smoke cleared above the battlefields, when the bills began to be presented. For services rendered, smashed pieces of Europe picked up in the war *débris* were being passed over the Peace Table to apply on account. All of the countries were there to collect. And great countries as easily elbowed lesser ones aside as the strong always crowd out the weak at any department store sale. Indeed, if you were a small country, you were fortunate not to be yourself casually snatched up and laid out like loot for some great country to incorporate within its enlarged boundaries. If you were a very little country, you knew better than to have any ambitions about being larger. You were properly grateful if they'd just give you a few materials with which to repair your shot-to-pieces, damaged and devastated little old land. For relief of this sort, there were standing in line some of the ablest diplomats the courts of Europe could send.

And then as I watched the spectacle from the windows of the Hotel Crillon, it had occurred. Looking backward even now, only the other day, it seems, that vision I glimpsed of a woman walk-

ing from out the war clouds. Right down the
steps of a throne she had come trippingly. And
she stepped straight out into the broad highway of
life where a journalist walks. One day she passed
my way so close, I signalled her excitedly. And
she had turned and waved gayly back to me, then
went on her way for that she had come to do.
Soon she was being tendered the hospitality of all
nations at Paris. The newspapers were chroni-
cling teas and luncheons and dinners and every
fête you can think of given in her honor by princes
and premiers and presidents and all sorts of prom-
inent plenipotentiaries. And Queen Marie had
taken the limelight "to give her country a face in
the affairs of the world," as she so naïvely announced. It was from that historical moment that
Roumania began to widen its way on the map.

I watched the drama unfold. It was the more
conspicuous because the leading lady was the only
lady in it. Though there were no women wanted
for the making of the peace, just one had come.
And lo, the skill with which she woman-handled
that distinguished gathering of black-frocked
delegates in international conference assembled.
Such clever technique! Such feminine charm!

You see, Roumania, being such a little land and
a far off one, wasn't getting proper attention amid
the universal babel of demand. The prestige of
this country as an Ally in regular standing was
questioned by some: the office boy or the usher or
somebody like that for the Hall of Mirrors had

rather flippantly received the cards of the Roumanian delegation and shown the gentlemen to a
seat rather far down the Peace Table. Then, when
they had presented their bill of particulars for
winning the war, its items were challenged. Anyhow, see the truce they had made with the Germans!

That was the way the conference was acting.
Even the Red Cross, sending out new missions of
assistance for war-racked lands, was always busy.
Or it slipped by on the other side of the Boulevard. Everybody had been so eager to get Roumania into the war. But who would now get her
out?

And it was due to that dilemma that the Queen
of Roumania was registered at the Ritz Hotel. We
sat on a sofa there one day, Her Majesty and I,
and it was as woman to woman we talked. And
sometimes as woman to woman we laughed softly
together. "But however did you get here?" I had
asked.

"Well, you see, it was like this," she explained.
"From over there at Bucharest in my far country,
I looked across to Paris where they were dividing
up Europe. And I realized, if we were to get our
share, somebody'd have to go get it. 'I'm going,'
I said to Ferdinand. He was quite appalled.
'My dear,' he declared, 'war time's no time for a
woman to be going about the world alone.' The
Prime Minister, too, demurred. Were not af-
fairs of state his affairs? But I just waved them

267

both aside. 'Gentlemen,' I said, 'leave it to me. I am a woman bound by no government vows. There are things I can do for Roumania that neither of you can. Gentlemen,' I said, 'leave it to me.' "

So the Queen had ordered her maid of honor to have the heavy trunks packed. And of course the hat boxes too. And she put on all of her pearls. Like that she had arrived at the Ritz and taken a large enough suite: some twenty rooms were stretching beyond this in which we sat. Here her ladies-in-waiting hung up and spread out all of her accoutrement. Not the Queen of Sheba, I am sure, was more splendidly outfitted. Still, this was Paris. So Marie shopped a day or so and got a few things more, as any woman would, you know. Finally, she let the Peace Conference know she had arrived. At Versailles, of course, there was not a vacant seat. But there were gentlemen who shoved back their chairs and jumped eagerly to their feet, when somebody exclaimed, "Look who's now in Paris!"

Why, she didn't even need to go to Versailles. They came to the Ritz. One by one they came and bowed before her and kissed her hand. Never mind the peace table. Give her a dinner table, a lunch table, a garden table instead. At these she did her work.

With such careful feminine forethought she had planned for it all ahead. There were in all some sixty gowns, thirty-one coats, twenty-two fur pieces, twenty-nine hats, and eighty-three pairs of slippers. "Perhaps it seems a good many," said the Queen. "Still, I feel that this is no time to economize. You see, Roumania simply has to have Transylvania. We want so much Bessarabia too. And what if for the lack of a gown, a concession should be lost?" Then a lady-in-waiting brought out the gowns, which were passed in review before us. The Queen commented: "This little gown trimmed with Point de Milan was for the reception at the Italian Embassy. That canary yellow silk proved just the thing when the Chinese Ambassador entertained in my honor. The white satin, edged with ermine, I wore at Buckingham Palace the week I was called over for a conference in England. And now do see," she pointed out with enthusiasm, "this mousseline de soie with the hand-painted rosebuds. As soon as I glimpsed it at Jenny's, I felt it would be just what Mr. Lloyd George would like. The gown of cloth of gold with heavy gold embroidery I specially selected for the luncheon with your American President. The blue of France over a petticoat of silver brocade, I had to have of course for the Premier here." Well, for each gown like that, there was a reason. The entire wardrobe was carefully designed for the earnest purpose of saving Roumania at the Peace Conference.

M. Clemenceau was roaring in his rage against that country when the Queen had arrived to inquire what the trouble was all about. The old lion of France even snapped at her. "I don't like your Prime Minister," he bellowed.

"Perhaps then you'll find me more agreeable," she suggested, flashing a blue-eyed glance and a brilliant smile. He did. He did. So that soon the Supreme Council discovered that one nation had quite reversed its policy: here was France as warmly backing Roumania's claims as before she had opposed them.

The Americans meant not to be so easily taken. From European gentlemen who knew, they had heard the tradition current of the charm and the skill of the most beautiful woman in the world. One American there was who boasted that though she charmed the birds from the trees, he wouldn't be beguiled by her. Then he began to learn from his subordinates that somebody had heard the Queen of Roumania say how much she admired the man who was feeding Europe. Somebody said the Queen of Roumania had seen his photograph and gazing long and deep had murmured, "a real man; yes, a real man." Somebody had been told by somebody else that the Queen of Roumania had exclaimed, "He's such a great man, the man I'd rather meet than any other in Paris."

Did the gentleman, do you think, now wish to meet the Queen? Why, he came and saw and was conquered. The lady was one to make any man glad he came. Even the obdurate gentleman was glad. It was when she had him feeling that way, that she lifted ingenuous blue eyes. It could not be true, she felt sure, that Roumania was to be forgotten in the distribution of American relief. Surely that must be but an idle ugly rumor. There had been, she knew, some unpleasant oil complications. And of course the gentleman was interested in oil. But surely he wouldn't let anything like that stand in the way of the assistance her people so much needed. He was, she knew, altogether too big and too fine for anything like that.

Well, now, of course he was. And don't you suppose he proved it? Not merely in bushels. In tons and tons, relief rolled toward Roumania.

It was the President of the United States who held out longest. He struggled to maintain a distance that should be safe and sane. A government messenger was sent to carry his respects. He would like, of course, to call himself. But he was such a busy man and how could he? The only free moments he had away from the council of the nations were in the morning, which was scarcely the time for social calls. The President regretted, etc.

But the Queen only smiled and said how much she liked morning calls. Again the presidential messenger returned: it would have to be such an early morning call at, for her, such an inconvenient hour. And the President regretted and regretted, etc.

The imperturbable lady only replied that no hour could be an inconvenient hour. Her own day began at seven. From that hour on, she would be breakfasted, dressed, and ready to receive.

How could even a President regret any further?
He called at 9 A.M. And before he left, he was
pleased enough to ask for the honor of entertaining
the lady at a special luncheon. After that he was
not so busy. At some time or other, there was
written a check on the United States government
for a loan of $20,000,000 to Roumania.

By now the American Relief Administrator and
the American Red Cross had gallantly mobilized
all of their resources in the service of the Queen
of Roumania. Through her new agrarian legislation, her people, to be sure, had the land. But
more than two years' occupation by enemy in-
vaders had left them little else; until the next harvest, at least, they would require help. See how
it came. Day by day one began to read in the
newspapers: 3,000 tons of seed are on the way to
Roumania for spring planting; 900 tons of pow-
dered milk are going to Roumanian children; a
shipload of 20,000 tons of flour has just been landed
at Constanza; one day there was a final estimate
listing 230,000 tons of foodstuffs that had been
allotted to Roumania.

The society columns were spilling over with all
the honors that were being done a lady with a
Peace Conference at her feet. And invariably
after every reception or tea party or other pleasant
little social occasion, one read next day in the
papers that something nice for Roumania had
occurred. So many kind tokens of esteem were
being carefully collected by a very busy and very

beautiful Queen. Admiration by trainload and shipload and dollar sign had been most graciously received. But after all, the biggest business the Queen had come about was her boundaries. Her lost provinces were what she was looking for. Soon every diplomat in Paris was, too. Searching official inquiry was made at the Peace Table: had any country by mistake picked up territory belonging to this lady's land?

It was then that big burly countries began bringing it back, saying shamefacedly they could do without it—or somebody else could. Neatly wrapped packages kept coming from Versailles to be left on Her Majesty's doorstep at the Ritz Hotel all checked and labelled, "For Roumania." I think it was Bessarabia, I first noticed by the newspapers, that had been duly awarded by recommendation of the Supreme Council to Roumania.

It was wonderful how that Peace Conference was coming to terms. Just before the Queen had reached Paris a leading newspaper had commented: "The Allies are committing more than an injustice, they are committing a blunder when, owing to we do not know what financial influences or high political reasons, they assume against all Roumanian claims that hostile attitude which exasperates general opinion in Roumania." And Roumania, as we have seen, was getting scant attention. It was such a small country. Some didn't even know where it was on the map. No powerful country was at that time espousing its cause. Bullying ones were browbeating it out of every claim it presented. Bah! What had Roumania done to win the war?

Then, suddenly, the Queen in her beauty had come to tell them. Roumania was the land where soldiers had bared a naked breast to the enemy thrust that thus the others had escaped. It was nearly a million men who had given their lives in occupying the attention of powerful enemy divisions deflected from another front. And that German truce there would have been no need for had the pledged and promised assistance arrived. Why, it was not Roumania but the Allies themselves who had failed in allegiance!

So right about the Roumanian case was turned. All the peacemakers who listened and looked in the lady's eyes easily saw how wrong the Conference had been. Day by day now did the Hall of Mirrors echo with oratorical indignation at the way little Roumania had been betrayed and deserted in her hour of peril. Even an overwhelming sense of personal responsibility began to press heavily on the manly hearts. Where, oh, where had he himself been when this beautiful woman had come down the staircase at Jassy, alone and unprotected, to face a German general? That was what each began to feel. Ah, if but he might have been there in her defense! And what could he now do to atone!

Well, really. Out of her handbag, the lady whipped a secret treaty. It was the agreement concluded in August, 1916, between France, Great Britain, Italy, and Russia on the one part, and Roumania on the other part. Here were definitely outlined the conditions on which Roumania entered the war. "And, gentlemen," said the Queen, "I want the Greater Roumania my soldiers were promised they were fighting for."

When this treaty was spread on the Peace Table it was a completely docile Conference that viewed the exhibit. Everything had been a terrible mistake. And one who had been the least among the nations at Versailles suddenly became the most popular. Everybody loved Roumania now. Special messengers were summoned to follow fast on each other's heels. Bessarabia, the Bucovina, Transylvania and the Banat were in turn breathlessly delivered at the Ritz. And the newspapers of two continents awoke to the picture silhouetted against the European skyline—Lady carving out a Kingdom.

It was the Greater Roumania her soldiers had died for. The Queen had arrived at the Peace Conference from a kingdom numbering eight million subjects. She departed the ruler of eighteen million.

Of course as soon as she reached home, Her Majesty asked first about the children. And then, as she stood before the mirror removing her hat, "Nanda," she said complacently, "it's a good thing God gave me a personality that pleases people." And she told him all that had happened in Paris.

"My dear," assured the King as he kissed her, "you're the luck of the country!"

"The luck of the country," he repeated with satisfaction. And kissed her again.

CHAPTER XI

A Queen of Queens

WHAT kind of a Queen would Missy make? As the world came back to routine after the war, that was a question which more or less had agitated royal relatives throughout Europe.

Uneasily they were remembering how from the days when she had walked with her nurse in the Green Park, it had ever been difficult to hold the child to the gravel path. And as she grew up, it had been more and more apparent how she loved the by-ways and the new ways and most of all to make her own way in paths as yet untrod.

So Alphonse, the King of Spain, was sent down to Roumania with well-meant advice on behalf of all the royal connections. You see, among the courts of Europe it is Spain that has been always noted for the stiffest etiquette. All that is severest in form and ceremony has been embodied there in required court procedure at Madrid. Every one has always walked just so and moved just so and dressed just so, with every detail of precedent carefully worked out with the same nicety that also gravely determined how many angels could dance on the point of a needle. Spanish etiquette

277

long ago became the synonym for an elegance that the other courts of Europe have striven to emulate.

And to everybody, all the cousins and the uncles and the aunts, it seemed most important that Missy "way down there" should get the new court in line and started right. It was much to their chagrin then that the Queen of Roumania made light of this solemn matter presented by her elegant cousin, the reigning monarch of Spain. "My dear Alphonse," she answered merrily, "you belong to a reigning house that began God knows when. And you may have to have your kingdom as it has been handed down to you. But for me, I have no Velasquez. Mine is a dynasty that began but yesterday. This court is different from the other courts of Europe. I mean it shall be. Why be like others when one has a chance to start like one's self? Why copy when one can perfectly well originate?

"You see, my dear Alphonse," she complacently continued, "you have your compensations and I have mine. You have your many ancestral palaces and your ancient traditions. But I have no painted pictures of a long line of predecessors to stare at me from my walls. I can make my kingdom as I like it. You are looking backward. I look only forward. And I have my vision of the future and all the wonders that may be for a people who are just beginning to find their own soul."

Well, Alphonse had his answer to carry back to

the confusion of the others. Marie was flouting them all. "My kingdom," she ended finally, "faces the future. I shall not impose the past upon it— nor upon myself. I don't have to be the kind of Queen that Great Aunt Elizabeth was, any more than I have to wear a ruff like hers about my neck. I'm going to be exactly the kind of Queen that I want to be. And it won't be a wooden one."

They might have known it. Wasn't that Missy all over again! Something like a sigh swept through the kings' palaces of a continent. But they had not even then realized the full portent of this new platform of royal principles. It seemed only to forecast what they soon saw come to pass: the new court at Bucharest was going to be what you might call easy on ceremony. Everything, as Marie arranged, should be as simple as possible. "Just because I'm royalty," she declared, "I see no reason to swathe myself about in its musty out-worn habiliments."

So, from the first, there have been no "presenta-tion" occasions other than the court balls. Even these of late have been few and far between. "Why should I," says the Queen frankly, "be giving en-tertainments to feed people who already have so much more than they need to eat?" So usually now it is but a musicale that she gives, with no ex-tensive collation. There is really need, perhaps, for feeding people's souls. Besides, for a musicale, there can be such a wide-open invitation list. At Cotroceni even a school teacher may sit beside a princess to listen to Beethoven. "I like to mix them all up," says the Queen mischievously, "the sort of people who wouldn't expect to be speaking to each other, only that under my royal roof they have to."

Even for the most formal of court functions, the court ball, there are no mystifying requirements. Any guest may meet the sovereigns without intricate procedure or the least court order about the kind of garment to have on. There is but one condition—and that unwritten—to give you pause: for heaven's sake, be interesting. Or, well, you won't make a hit with Marie. She can't endure bores. You may be prince or potentate or king, and yet never really get by with the lady. Or you may be a painter of pictures, a singer of songs, a writer of stories, an American stage dancer, or a self-made business man from out of the west, and suddenly find yourself closer to a Queen than any of her class can come. It has happened so again and again to the puzzlement of aristocracy, nobility, and royalty, who have failed to possess that other accident of birth, personality, which is the highest claim of all to preferment.

I think the first time the royal discernment registered like this was years ago when Missy was yet but a new little bride in Bucharest. There had come a girl from Illinois, or maybe it was Iowa, dancing her way across the world to the stage of the Teatrul National on the Calea Victorei. The Crown Princess, a spectator from the royal box, sent up a warm and impulsive note, expressing her ardent admiration for the artistic exhibition. Such recognition meant even more then than it might now. In those days relatives of the dancer back in the state from which she had come sat in the family pew on Sunday, as it were, in sackcloth and ashes about a connection who had gone on the stage. It wasn't, you see, yet done in the best families. And this one didn't then realize how high on the road to fame was their relative. Of course in these later years they have come, along with everybody else, to feel quite differently. It's fine now to be identified by family ties with a woman recognized throughout the world as one of the great creators in modern terpsichorean art. All this, however, was still to come to pass, when there in Bucharest literally the applause of a generation was begun by the joyous outburst from one girl to another. That royal note that reached the stage performer commenced a correspondence which has not ceased and a friendship which all the years since have only cemented.

Democratic deviations in respect to personal preferences the other royalties have been prepared to expect in Marie. And they have long since been resigned to them as to the inevitable. But her democracy in politics and economics, that has indeed given all Europe new alarm. That agrarian law! "Why, oh, why did she do it?" kings have asked kings in querulous complaint. Especially is criticism stiff-lipped in those other lands over which the curse of unemployment hangs heavy to-day with the common people out of work, while thousands of acres are still withheld in the vast hunting preserves and parks of the idle rich. Among titled folk everywhere you will find mur-muring at the innovation so startlingly inaugurated way down there by the Danube. Shall a nation that has been supposed to be among the least of the kingdoms of a continent lead all the rest?

Then came Missy's Peace Conference proce-dure. Courts beyond Bucharest there were that felt the shock of the Queen's proposal when she waved all her ministers aside. "Never mind," she insisted to everybody, "you'll all just have to get used to accepting me with the faults of my virtues. If I've got courage, every little while I shall have also what you'll call daring. I'm not afraid even of mistakes. One who never makes them never makes anything else. Indeed, I believe there's nothing I'm going to like better than to hurl my-self head on now and then at a good mistake." But the Peace Conference adventure of the Queen of Roumania turned out an episode with so triumph-ant a conclusion that it must be condoned by the most censorious. If Marie had failed! But she has not the habit of failing.

After the war and the peace, there was Bol-shevism everywhere abroad in the land. So that in every palace it began to be felt that we kings and queens should certainly everywhere stand to-gether and be so careful. The concern of one is now more than ever the concern of all. An assassination anywhere might reverberate everywhere. Yet, in times like these, still see Missy. Why, everybody who went down there came back to tell with what naïveté she still goes about among her people. You may find her galloping away on her horse even as when she was a Crown Princess to visit with the shepherds on lonely mountain sides. Or, wearing their national costume, she sits with the country people in their humble cottages. Or she walks in the forests in her short swinging skirt with the free stride of a peasant girl. And when you consider what's happened to thrones, and the worst of all to one next door to hers! Oh, everybody nervously felt that somebody should do something about it.

So Alphonse was hurried down again. Earnestly he told Cousin Missy that this wasn't the way that Majesty should be done. "It is impossible, preposterous," he urged, "that you, a Queen, should go about where you will, alone and unattended. At least," he begged, "have a groom to accompany you as a personal guard."

But she shook her head. "I just don't have to, Alphonse," she said. "I love freedom of movement because it expresses my freedom of soul. That's the way God made me. And that's the way I'm going to continue to be. It's no use for you to try to change me. You'd spoil me if you did. And you yourselves wouldn't find me satisfactory. Besides, many people like me very well as I am.

And because of this, I find them ready to do things for me and for Roumania."

It was useless for him to protest. "No," she insisted firmly. "I'll be a Queen all right. And I'll be it splendidly. For that's the way I believe Queens ought to be. But besides, all the while too, I shall go right on being a human being. I am content to be in the hands of God." And again she repeated what is the most characteristically far-flung slogan of her soul: "I am never afraid!"

Isn't that a Queen for these difficult days! Still with all her personal democracy, you should know that beneath it is a royalty that is racial. "Once," says the Queen of Roumania, "somebody said to me, 'But you've never been down in the street. That is, for all of your flitting about, you've never been down there to stay. So how should you know about life? Most of all, about regulating it for others?'

"Now that, I pointed out," says the Queen, "is just the reason. To have been brought up amid the special and beautiful surroundings afforded for royalty must inevitably give a special color and line to one's thought that the workaday man and woman cannot possess. It's because I've never been jostled and knocked about that I can have the point of view required for a ruler. What I mean is, that all there is of me can be used for vision. I am not having to struggle against the crowd to keep my foothold, because I hold that by birth. I have never been obliged to spend my energy and

strength, my life force, in arriving. I was born
to a high place. Others must climb to it. And
in that struggle to attain, something corroding may
happen to the soul.

"It must be very difficult to escape a bitterness.
I don't know how you are going to escape a bitterness that must come into the heart against those
who would pull you back, who would even trample
you down that they may pass you to the goal. You
see, there is jealousy. And there is hate. These
are the two great poisons of the body and the soul.
And there is love, the great creative force, the re-
deeming force of the world. Now, you see, I don't
have to hate and to be jealous, as if I were one of
the herd. By just so much, then, I have a better
chance to express love. And the ability to express
love, I believe, is the measure of the greatness of
any ruler."

Well, so here you have the royalty that she is
and the democracy that she does. It is through
them both that she is making this ancient land a
modern one and lifting it to its new high place
among the nations. Throughout her country there
is an ever increasing hum of activity. On the
horizon the oil derricks rise ever blacker. Bucharest bustles breathlessly to expand for all the
new commerce that crowds its cobble-stoned
streets. The narrow sidewalks spill over with
people. On the Calea Victorei the throngs press
as on Fifth Avenue or Oxford Street. And for a
new world impinging directly on the old, see in

the Strada Salculor the Roumanian Y.M.C.A.
headquarters under the direction of William H.
Morgan, from Union, South Carolina. It was up
at Jassy the Queen first saw him, when one day he
gave out four thousand cups of tea to her famished
and frozen soldiers. "I want that young man," she
said with conviction. Then when she was getting
her new kingdom in order after the peace, she
came back one time from a trip to Paris bringing
with her an American delegation to organize for
Roumania a Y.W.C.A. In a Roumanian residence of Arabesque architecture you find it func-
tioning to-day as busily as in any brick building
on Main Street in America. Down the long hall-
way past the ikon's niche, if you follow the fragrant odor of the green peppers that season all Roumanian cooking, you will come upon the dining
room recently turned into a cafeteria for the Roumanian working girl just now arriving in industry. What do the Roumanian ladies know about
her? Well, from the wife of Commander Pantazzi of the Roumanian navy, they can learn:
Ethel Greening Pantazzi, who came from her
birthplace in Canada to live since her marriage in
the lovely white house set in a garden within an
old courtyard off the street of the Holy Apostles.
How it is done in America she can tell them. And
the secretary knows, Christine Galitzei. With her
eastern beauty and white crystalline quality of
soul, see Christine Galitzei, born in Roumania of
Greek parents, educated in a French school in

Constantinople, later a graduate at the Sorbonne and finally a post graduate with an A.M. degree from Columbia University in New York. So now from this very old city by the Dumbavitza, Y.M. and Y.W. summer camps are organizing social life for young men and young women. Gymnasiums are teaching them games and athletics. Country branches are carrying hygiene and child culture to peasant villages. Committees are meeting. Classes are organizing. Conferences are assembling, even as in New York or Chicago or in Union, South Carolina. Still the beggars in Bucharest sun themselves along the sidewalks, hands uplifted in prayer in their old futile, feudal gesture. But on an ancient religion of worship is being grafted to-day a new religion of social service. And a civilization whose builder and maker is a Queen is bringing a Christianity that is for here, as well as for heaven.

A wide diversity of interests engages the attention of this sovereign. Not always is she cheerleading a nation at war or smiling a peace conference into submission. She also serves her state, you see, in other ways. It may be in the development of everyday religion or in the encouragement of silk culture or in the renewal of Roumanian art. Nothing that may concern the most commonplace or the most cultural need of her people fails of appeal to her. She is, I think you would say, always busy about being a Queen. And though she is literally the most important woman of a continent, even for her there are personal and domestic details that crowd close on statecraft. Would you visualize a royal calendar? Perhaps a day that I witnessed is as typical as any. See how it goes. Her mail this morning is very deep. She has even come to breakfast, a letter in hand. It is, she told us all, from Mignon. And the baby Peter, heir to the Serbian throne, has triumphantly achieved a new tooth. As she drinks her coffee, her secretary breaks in with a press telegram relayed from a morning newspaper in Bucharest. And she reads with satisfaction that Russian Soviet activities in Bessarabia are under control.

Right after breakfast, the day's schedule starts. A housemaid is going to be married and she must be interested in that. There is a new chef in the kitchen who must be talked to personally about the soup. It is made from a recipe that was her mother's. And it is the most perfect soup in the world when properly put together. There are exact instructions for the chef. Does he feel surely that he can do it? The chef bows very low and feels that he can. "Though really," she has told me, "I should like myself to have gone to the kitchen."

After the chef, there is the architect who waits with plans for a new royal residence. He is admitted with his blueprints. She looks them critically over. "For that particular wall," she points out, "it is the Gothic line that is required. The rest will do very well. Only be careful, please, about my windows."

There's a church to be dedicated with her admiration. She talks with a priest who comes about that. An oil monopoly wants her ear: she listens well to the American gentleman. But the beautiful face that's made a little land a large one remains just smiling, inscrutable.

Then there comes a Roumanian statesman whom she herself has summoned. Here is the most critical interview of all. Not the man before her alone must be handled; there is another to be reached through him. It was an English diplomat, as she afterwards explained to me, who was about to make a move that would have been an international catastrophe. What was impending had reached Her Majesty from a long way around through the secret channels of statecraft. The English proposal must be stopped at all hazards.

She looks into the eyes of the man before her and smiles charmingly, engagingly. Now, while the English effort couldn't possibly be permitted the way that it was started, still if its promoter could be induced to turn his plan right the other way around . . . so then it could safely go through without throwing out of gear all the machinery of the Roumanian state, together with that of some four or five neighboring principalities.

But the English diplomat must be so carefully approached. She may not herself warn him. Can she trust the man before her with this delicate mission? She smiles and smiles some more. She smokes a cigarette or two with him. Again she looks in his eyes. Now he is ready. Yes, now it may be done.

So she tells him. And her surmise is correct. He will be most happy to serve in this so strategic emergency. As he bows himself out, she throws herself exhausted among the divan's precious pillows.

"But," she exclaims to me, "I have saved just now, for the moment at least, perhaps the peace of central Europe."

Nor is it infrequently there is drama like this in her day. Through it all, she works very quietly but very industriously. She makes no speeches in public; she makes them so well in private. You recall the statesmen who came to Bran? It is the methods she used with them that invariably prevail. She has smiled. A gentleman has kissed her hand. And a measure of state is on the way. Comes a day when it is consummated at last. Some one thinks he did it, a senator, a Prime Minister, a King, a Crown Council, or perhaps it is a whole Parliament of men. That's the way she lets them feel. Brilliant minds! She applauds. Their names get written in government reports. History will take care of hers. Though on the stage of Roumanian political affairs the lady has not appeared at all, yet, listen! From the wings there is sometimes the swish of a red kilted skirt, the echo of a woman's soft laughter.

It is clever everyday effacement like this which makes the more spectacular the occasions when the Queen of Roumania takes the world's spotlight. And watch! Is the lady who has carved out a kingdom now laying the lines of an empire? Beyond her already Greater Roumania lies all central and southeastern Europe, where wider territory unrolls. It is very like a Federation of States way down there, which she already holds within the radius of her charm. They call her the "soul of the Little Entente" and "the brains of the Balkans." Within one or both of these groups or close to them are included: Roumania; Czecho Slovakia; Jugo-Slavia, which now means the Serbs, Croats, and Slovenes; Montenegro; Macedonia and Dalmatia; Greece; Albania and Poland. Not all of these are monarchies now. But suppose that some day Greece should recall King George and his consort Elizabeta, the daughter whom the Queen of Roumania set upon that throne. Alexander Karageorovitch, King of Serbia, who married her second daughter, is his mother-in-law's devoted admirer. "I want my Queen to be exactly like you," he assured her the day he secured from her a list of "Do's and Don'ts, for Mignon." As for Bulgaria, the King of that country has more than once sought in marriage the hand of a daughter of the Queen of Roumania; almost any daughter would do if he might but succeed. Albania

so much approves of this royal house that it has
considered offering its throne to the lady's second
son. Even a proletariat President of Poland said
to her: "Now, of course, if we could but have a
Queen like you;" his glance strayed to the Princess
Ileana, but it returned to the lovely face of Ileana's
mother.

Such is the supremacy of a personality that but
beckons and nations wish to follow. Not only
little ones. The lady who holds the Carpathians
has more than once been able to sway the Court of
St. James or the Quai d'Orsay in behalf of difficult Balkan situations. To-day not only in her
corner of the world is her preëminence recognized,
but a continent acclaims her. On the occasions of
her appearance in the capitals of Europe the people press and crowd for a glimpse of her. At the
opera in Paris they salute her, Vive la Reine.
Governments everywhere receive her with pomp
and splendor organized for the occasion of her
state visits. They greet her in court dress and gold
laced uniforms. They make magnificent reviews
and march their soldiers in dress parade before
her. They bring up their tanks and flame-throwing
sections and send up their battle planes to the sky
and show off all of their military machinery for
her entertainment. They make brilliant receptions
and gorgeous balls for her and banquet her at state
dinners off their best gold plate.

Why all of these maneuvers? You hear of
them for no other monarch. Ah, maybe it is more

than Roumania the lady has given a face. It seems it is the age she has given a face, the most beautiful one of its time. Is there any other more pictured in print to-day? When all of the movie stars shall have faded in the films of a bygone century, here is a face that will be fixed in the firmament of history. And for the present it holds the front pages of the newspapers of two continents. There is no city editor anywhere, from all the Morning Bulletins and Evening Standards among us to the London Times and the Echo de Paris and the Berliner Tageblatt who does not keep right at hand the latest cut of the Queen of Roumania. In Bucharest there is almost what you might call an organized industry to supply the world-wide post card demand. For two busy days I watched a photographer who came to Bran make more than two hundred plate exposures for post card pictures of Her Majesty. This same photographer comes four times a year, as do also three others from Bucharest. They each require a series to be issued regularly summer and winter, spring and fall, in four editions each year. These are reproduced in millions and millions of post cards placed on sale in the shop windows of the world. And such is the demand that not infrequently a last edition is sold out before the next can get printed.

Not since Catherine of Russia and Maria Theresa of Austria and Victoria of England, has there been a queen whose personality has so stamped a state. Not since Helen of Troy and

Cleopatra has there been a woman more silhouetted against her day. But all those are far away
and gone before. Here is a woman not yet a
myth or a statue in stone in a public square. She
is a living woman, the loveliness of whom and the
charm of whom illumines her own century.

Like that they crowned her, already enthroned
before the footlights of an admiring world. The
war and its vicissitudes had delayed the ceremony
until several years after the reign had begun. On
October 15, 1922, the coronation of Ferdinand I.
of Roumania, and Marie his consort, occurred.
The King in a robe of red velvet edged with ermine
was crowned with that same crown made from the
cannon of Plevna which Carol, the first King of
Roumania, had worn. But for the Queen there was
a quite new crown. Hers she carefully copied
from the crown of that Despina Doamna, the wife
of a Prince of Wallachia, whom you may see to-
day pictured in the frescoes of the ancient church
of Curtea de Arges. It is in weight four pounds
of the purest, yellowest gold of her own Transylvania, and set with moonstones, amethysts, turquoises, emeralds, and rubies. And she had the
loveliest gown of gold tissue, all of threads of pure
Transylvania gold. Her robe, too, was of gold,
edged with ermine. The entire costume was the
gift of her people. When they came to her about
it, she had said: "Do yourselves the honor to
give me that which best represents your own ancient Roumania. I want nothing modern that an-

other Queen might have. Let mine be all medieval."

And that was the keynote for the coronation occasion. It was a colorful pageant that was staged in a very old city that had been founded by Trajan. Mihai Bessarab, known in history as Mihai the Brave, in 1599 when he had formed the first union of the Roumanian Principalities, had made his triumphal entry there. So now this Alba Julia in the recently restored Transylvania was certainly the most fitting place in the kingdom for crowning the sovereigns who again after all the centuries are reigning over a once more united Roumania. The ancient cathedral had long ago been destroyed by the vandalism of the conquerors who had held the country in their power. But on its same site now had been specially erected for this occasion a new cathedral, as magnificently Byzantine, however, as any of Roumania's historic church edifices. Around it, the ancient little town of some six thousand population had been made all splendid for the great days, with the brilliant rugs that hung from every house window. The coronation service opened with solemn mass in the beautiful cathedral. The procession that issued forth was led by the Metropolitan and the Bishops in rich religious robes. Then came the sovereigns and the royal family and entourage followed by the foreign delegations. In the center of the public square, on a specially erected dais covered with rare carpets, the King and the Queen took their places.

A grandstand about the square was filled with high personages. Peasants in embroidered costumes were densely packed together filling every open space. No less than two hundred thousand people had come on pilgrimage for this day that symbolized the realization of the hope of centuries. Amid a reverential silence the Metropolitan held out the crown which the King received and placed on his own head. The voices of the heralds proclaiming his sovereignty thrilled out to the assembled throng. Now the Queen kneeling before her liege lord, he placed her crown also on her head. A chorus burst out in song. Representatives from all the nations of Christendom came forward to present their compliments. There was a state luncheon, after which the coronation party departed for Bucharest. Entering the capital by way of the Chausee Kisselef, beneath a massive arch of triumph, the King was offered by the municipal council the traditional bread and salt. On the procession moved to the Metropole for another church service. In the afternoon there were tableaux portraying phases in the country's history. At night there was a state dinner and brilliant receptions to the foreign ministers and diplomatic corps. The coronation occasion ended next day with a banquet to ten thousand mayors who arrived from all over the kingdom to do obeisance to their sovereigns. No effort had been spared to make the ceremonies all glorious for Roumania. The expense of the festivities amounted approximately to a million dollars.

So Marie of Roumania had arrived at the place the ages had prepared for her. I stood one day with her on a high mountain peak in old Moldavia. We looked down on the wide spreading land that swept away and away, into her Greater Roumania. "I am a winner in life," she said softly. Then, "Somebody has to lose," she added not unkindly but even regretfully. "But I am a winner in life." So to one of the smallest lands of her day she came, now to stand forth at last a shining figure, the greatest Queen of her time.

But hear it told more tersely. There was the occasion of her triumphal procession on a visit of state as she passed through the streets of London in her native land. An Englishman of title, adjusting his monocle for a more critical survey, exclaimed with warmth: "By Jove I'm not much on women. But I'll say, there's one who is every inch a Queen!" Then an English bobby by his side, better phrasing public opinion, added earnestly, "Yes sir, I'll say she's a Queen as knocks the spots off all the others."